CHANAKYA NEETI

CHANAKYA NEETI

Verses of Wisdom

RUPA

Published by
Rupa Publications India Pvt. Ltd 2022
7/16, Ansari Road, Daryaganj
New Delhi 110002

Sales Centres:
Allahabad Bengaluru Chennai
Hyderabad Jaipur Kathmandu
Kolkata Mumbai

P-ISBN: 978-93-5520-852-1
E-ISBN: 978-93-5520-853-8

First impression 2022

10 9 8 7 6 5 4 3 2 1

Printed in India

CONTENTS

1. Introduction 7

2. From the Neeti 13

3. Chanakya Sutras 85

INTRODUCTION

Chandragupta Maurya (321–297 BC), who founded the Mauryan Empire (322–185 BC), appointed Chanakya, also known by the names Kautilya or Vishnugupta (350–275 BC) as his prime minister. The political book *Arthashastra*, which Chanakya composed as a detailed manual on how to rule successfully for the youthful Chandragupta, is what he is best known for.

Chanakya was raised in Taxila and was a Brahmin by birth. He is thought to have excelled in the disciplines of medicine and astrology and was knowledgeable on Persian and Greek concepts that the Zoroastrians brought to India. It is debatable if he adhered to Zoroastrianism or was merely deeply impacted by it.

Since no historical texts from the Mauryan Empire have remained, only tales from diverse traditions provide information on his life's course. He appeared to have worked as an advisor for Dhanananda (329–322 BC), the last ruler of the Nanda Dynasty (343–321 BC), who controlled the Kingdom of Magadha, going with one of the probable theories.

According to a different theory, he was a Vedic scholar from the university at Taxila who visited the court of Dhanananda and was insulted during an almsgiving ceremony. He then completely dedicated himself to overthrowing the king. The king's son, Pabbata, was urged to join the cause. Chanakya recruited others before settling on Pabbata and Chandragupta, a young man who belonged to either the lower classes of the noble house or was a commoner, as the most plausible candidates. Chandragupta outperformed Pabbata in terms of skills and abilities, and Chanakya concentrated his efforts on grooming him as the prospective successor monarch over the following seven to nine years. When Chandragupta's training was complete, he deposed Dhanananda and took over as ruler of Magadha.

Innumerable compilations and anthologies have accumulated Chanakya's diverse theories about existence over time. If the lore is to be trusted, these theories were collected to honour the successful plan that put Chandragupta Maurya on the throne. The name *Chanakya Niti* refers to the entire corpus.

The aphorisms, which are still remembered throughout India, are fundamentally about ordinary life: about friends and enemies in the neighbourhood, wealth and wisdom, and the ultimate end of everything. They also provide guidance on the good and bad aspects of life, appropriate and inappropriate behaviour, and how to handle any challenging circumstances.

This Neeti gives rise to *Arthashastra*, which is revered as Chanakya's manual for turning Chandragupta from a prospective king into a monarch. As an Indian treatise on politics, economics, military strategy, the role of the state and social organization, the literature promotes taking direct action to handle political issues without giving much thought to moral issues. The text's aim is to provide a thorough understanding of statecraft to help a monarch rule successfully. The title is a combination of the Sanskrit words 'artha' (aim) and 'shastra' (treatise). The title has therefore been translated to *The Science of Politics*, *The Science of Political Economy*, and *The Science of Material Gain*; artha, in Hinduism, is understood as one of the fundamental aims of humans for pursuing wealth and social status.

By applying the *Arthashastra* doctrines, Chandragupta was able to conquer the kingdom, rule over it and eventually transfer his power to his son Bindusara (297–273 BC) and his grandson Ashoka the Great (268–232 BC). Until he became disillusioned by the battle and turned to Buddhism, some of Ashoka's early successes could be credited to *Arthashastra*. The literature belongs to the Charvaka school of philosophy, which was founded around 600 BC and rejected the supernatural aspects of faith in favour of a wholly materialistic understanding of the universe and life. Charvaka emphasized a practical approach to life that encompassed rational and reason-driven action as a response to every situation since it believed that only a firsthand perception of any given situation could establish the truth. *Arthashastra* takes the same approach when addressing issues like when and how a king should execute family members or competitors, how one should regard foreign states as enemies that are competing for the same resources and power, and how to most successfully neutralize them. After seizing control, Chanakya established strict administrative ethics combined with a complex system for the weak and oppressed to get social security. Without Charvaka's platform to build on, *Arthashastra*'s practical, hands-on approach is likely to never have been established.

Based on references to the arthashastras (plural) in works like the Mahabharata, it is believed that the concepts expressed in *Arthashastra* were drawn from previous books that are now forgotten. Although there is no scholarly unanimity to this assertion, it is impossible to compare the latest work to the alleged earlier versions. Furthermore, the concept of 'artha' encompasses more than just the fifteen volumes of *Arthashastra*'s fifteen chapters on politics, military strategy, economics, animal husbandry, marriage and other disciplines. The quest for material wealth, prosperity, stability and social prestige are all examples of artha. There is consequently no need to assume that the current book is only a modification of earlier works. Similar alleged early arthashastras may have dealt with any wide range of subjects along these lines, quite possibly including politics.

Even after Ashoka's rule, *Arthashastra* remained one of the most influential works, but for a while it was thought to be lost before being found in 1905 by the Sanskrit scholar Rudrapatna Shamasastry (1868–1944). He first published the work in 1909, and then after translating it to English in 1915, published a fresh edition that made the text famous.

The Prince by Niccolò Machiavelli (1469–1527)—whose book on how a Renaissance prince should rule became as important in Europe as *Arthashastra* was in India over 1500 years earlier—is widely studied alongside this text as one of the finest political discourses ever written. *Arthashastra* was founded on the same tenet as *The Prince*, which is that a great leader is someone who can see what needs to be done and can accomplish it, regardless of morals. It has moreover been compared with Sun Tzu's *The Art of War* and Plato's *Republic* as a guide for creating and sustaining a powerful State.

It is reasonable to assume that these thoughts possess the fundamental power to alter not just one's state of mind but also one's course in life as a whole. Chanakya stands out from other great thinkers and philosophers for his witty and forthright ideas for and on life, which contrast with the positive outlook that others have attempted to present for living a full life. These were, and still are, the teachings that have persisted through the test of time and space.

The core of Chanakya's philosophy is reality. In order to climb above and ultimately beyond it, the facts of life and society should be centred. In the book *Chanakya Niti*, his reflections on life and the universe are captured. People adopt his teachings to break free from the chain of societal evils and live happy, tranquil lives. He recorded his findings in order to serve as a benchmark for how people should have lived in ancient India. The book describes the behaviours and patterns that, when adopted while taking in mind the various personalities of individuals, can result in success and prosperity.

Some of the shlokas from the book have been reproduced here:

Yaddeechchasi Vasheekartu Jagadeken Karmana.
Paraapavaadashaastreebhyo Gaam Charanteem Nivaarya.

If one wants to overpower the world through actions, then restraint should be practiced upon speech. Harsh and bitter language can cause irreparable damage which can prove to be more harmful than the pain from a fire burn.

Shaantitullyam Tapo Naasti Na Santoshaatparamsukham.
Na Trishnayaaparo Vyaadhirnacha Dharmo Dayaaparah.

No penance is greater than the one practiced to preserve peace, no peace is better than the one attained through contentment, no disease is as destructive as greed, and no dharma is better than having compassion for all.

Anaagat vidhaataa Cha Prattutpannamatistathaa.
Dvaavetau Sukhameveta Yaddbhavishyo Vinashyati.

He who is aware of future troubles and possesses wit will

remain happy. In contradiction to this stage, he who remains sedentary, waiting for the good days to come ruins his own life.

FROM THE NEETI

On Society and Family

Chanakya established a number of fundamental principles that a society and its members should go by because he was conscious of the community he wanted to be a part of. He believed that the safety of the population was of utmost importance. He was in favour of all forms of agriculture and thought that it was a thing that concerned the State. He put land on a vital pedestal as a resource and so advocated for its optimal utilization. He took excellent care of the resources of the annexed empires and kingdoms in order to maximize their potential.

He was an advocate for safeguarding women from all types of exploitation. He struck a balance between the State and its citizens as he was a strategist. He wanted trade to prosper and hence advocated for the imposition of the fewest possible taxes that would benefit both the State and the people. He advocated the construction of forts to deter foreign invasion and intended to develop cities for trade both inside and beyond the State.

The qualities that the head of the household should possess have also been highlighted in *Chanakya Niti* in order to prevent any basic problems from harming the family and its members. He asserted that the family patriarch ought to reject any belief that lacks solid evidence. Any news must be verified before being accepted. A gullible person who blindly believes all others say may cause serious issues for the family.

The head of the family must exercise prudent financial management. A lot of frivolous spending can send the incorrect message to the family and lead to financial difficulties. There won't ever be money problems in the family if the head of the household learns how to manage money and starts saving. Savings are crucial to surviving harsh times. The family head should consider the opinions of each member before making a choice that will benefit everyone. They must adhere to decisions if he or she wants to foster a culture of discipline in the household.

❖

यस्मिन्देशे न सम्मानो न वृत्तिर्न च बान्धवाः।
न च विद्यागमोऽप्यस्ति वासं तत्र न कारयेत्।।

Yasmindeśe Na Sammāno Na Vṛttirna Ca Bāndhavāḥ.
Na Cha Vidyāgamo'pyasti Vāsaṃ Tatra Na Kārayet.

A country where a person is not respected, cannot earn livelihood, has no friends or cannot acquire knowledge should not be inhabited.

यथा चतुर्भिः कनकं परीक्ष्यते निघर्षणच्छेदनतापताडनैः ।
तथा चतुर्भिः पुरुषः परीक्ष्यते त्यागेन शीलेन गुणेन कर्मणा ।।

Yathā Caturbhiḥ Kanakaṃ Parīkṣyate
Nigharṣaṇacchedanatāpatāḍanaiḥ.
Tathā Caturbhiḥ Puruṣaḥ Parīkṣyate
Tyāgena Śīlena Guṇena Karmaṇā.

Gold is tested in four ways: by rubbing, cutting, heating and beating. A man should be tested similarly through his renunciation, conduct, qualities and actions.

मुक्तिमिच्छसि चेत्तात विषयान्विषवत्त्यज ।
क्षमार्जवदयाशौचं सत्यं पीयूषवत्पिब ।।

Muktimicchasi Cettāta Viṣayānviṣavattyaja.
Kṣamārjavadayāśaucaṃ Satyaṃ Pīyūṣavatpiba.

If one desires to get free from the cycle of birth and death, then the objects of sensual gratification have to be abandoned like poison. Instead, the nectar of forbearance, upright conduct, mercy, cleanliness and truth should be drunk.

धनिकः श्रोत्रियो राजा नदी वैद्यस्तु पञ्चमः ।
पञ्च यत्र न विद्यन्ते न तत्र दिवसं वसेत् ।।

Dhanikaḥ Śrotriyo Rājā Nadī Vaidyastu Pañcamaḥ.
Pañca Yatra Na Vidyante Na Tatra Divasaṃ Vaset.

Do not, even a single day, stay at a place where there are not these five persons: a wealthy man, a well-versed brahmana in Vedic lore, a king, a river and a physician.

न विश्वसेत्कुमित्रे च मित्रे चापि न विश्वसेत् ।
कदाचित्कुपितं मित्रं सर्वं गुह्यं प्रकाशयेत् ।।

Na Viśvasetkumitre Ca Mitre Cāpi Na Viśvaset.
Kadācitkupitaṃ Mitraṃ Sarvaṃ Guhyaṃ Prakāśayet.

Do not trust a bad companion or even an ordinary friend, for if they get angry with you, they might bring all your secrets to light.

मनसा चिन्तितं कार्यं वाचा नैव प्रकाशयेत् ।
मन्त्रेण रक्षयेद्गूढं कार्ये चापि नियोजयेत् ।।

Manasā Cintitaṃ Kāryaṃ Vācā Naiva Prakāśayet.
Mantreṇa Rakṣayedgūḍhaṃ Kārye Cāpi Niyojayet.

Do not reveal what you have thought of doing. By wise council, keep it a secret while considering carrying it to execution.

कान्तावियोगः स्वजनापमानं ऋणस्य शेषं कुनृपस्य सेवा ।
दारिद्र्यभावाद्विमुखं च मित्रं विनाग्निना पञ्च दहन्ति कायम् ।।

Kāntāviyogaḥ Svajanāpamānaṃ
Ṛṇasya Śeṣaṃ Kunṛpasya Sevā.
Dāridryabhāvādvimukhaṃ Ca Mitraṃ
Vināgninā Pañca Dahanti Kāyam.

Separation from wife, disgrace from one's own people, an enemy saved in battle, service to a wicked ruler, poverty and a mismanaged assembly. These six evils, if afflicting a person, can burn him without fire.

लोकयात्रा भयं लज्जा दाक्षिण्यं त्यागशीलता ।
पञ्च यत्र न विद्यन्ते न कुर्यात्तत्र संस्थितिम् ।।

Lokayātrā Bhayaṃ Lajjā Dākṣiṇyaṃ Tyāgaśīlatā.
Pañca Yatra Na Vidyante Na Kuryāttatra Saṃsthitim.

Wise men should never visit a country where there are no means of earning a livelihood, where people do not dread anyone and have no sense of shame, intelligence or a charitable disposition.

वरं वनं व्याघ्रगजेन्द्रसेवितं द्रुमालयं पत्रफलाम्बुसेवनम् ।
तृणेषु शय्या शतजीर्णवल्कलं न बन्धुमध्ये धनहीनजीवनम् ।।

Varaṃ Vanaṃ Vyāghragajendrasevitaṃ
Drumālayaṃ Patraphalāmbusevanam.

Tṛṇeṣu Śayyā Śatajīrṇavalkalaṃ
Na Bandhumadhye Dhanahīnajīvanam.

It should be preferred to live under a tree in a jungle inhabited by tigers and elephants to maintain oneself in such a place with ripe fruits and spring water, to lie down on the grass and to wear the ragged barks of trees than to live among relatives when one is reduced to poverty.

आत्मवर्गं परित्यज्य परवर्गं समाश्रयेत् ।
स्वयमेव लयं याति यथा राजान्यधर्मतः ।।

Ātmavargaṃ Parityajya Paravargaṃ Samāśrayet.
Svayameva Layaṃ Yāti Yathā Rājānyadharmataḥ.

The person who forsakes their own community and joins another perishes as the king who embraces an unrighteous path.

सानन्दं सदनं सुतास्तु सुधियः कान्ता प्रियालापिनी
इच्छापूर्तिधनं स्वयोषिति रतिः स्वाज्ञापराः सेवकाः ।
आतिथ्यं शिवपूजनं प्रतिदिनं मिष्टान्नपानं गृहे
साधोः संगमुपासते च सततं धन्यो गृहस्थाश्रमः ।।

Sānandaṃ Sadanaṃ Sutāstu Sudhiyaḥ Kāntā Priyālāpinī
Icchāpūrtidhanaṃ Svayoṣiti Ratiḥ Svājñāparāḥ Sevakāḥ.
Ātithyaṃ Śivapūjanaṃ Pratidinaṃ Miṣṭānnapānaṃ Gṛhe
Sādhoḥ Saṃgamupāsate Ca Satataṃ Dhanyo Gṛhasthāśramaḥ.

He is a blessed householder in whose house there is positive atmosphere, whose sons are skilled, whose wife is soft-spoken, whose wealth is enough to satisfy his worldly needs, who finds pleasure in the company of his wife, whose servants are obedient, hospitality is shown in whose house and the auspicious Supreme Lord is worshiped daily, delicious food and drink is partaken, and who finds joy in the company of devotees.

कष्टं च खलु मूर्खत्वं कष्टं च खलु यौवनम् ।
कष्टात्कष्टतरं चौव परगेहनिवासनम् ।।

Kaṣṭaṃ Ca Khalu Mūrkhatvaṃ Kaṣṭaṃ Ca Khalu Yauvanam.
Kaṣṭātkaṣṭataraṃ Caiva Paragehanivāsanam.

Foolishness is painful, and verily so is youth, but more painful by far than either is being obligated to survive in another person's house.

शैले शैले च माणिक्यं मौक्तिकं न गजे गजे ।
साधवो न हि सर्वत्र चन्दनं न वने वने ।।

Śaile Śaile Ca Māṇikyaṃ Mauktikaṃ Na Gaje Gaje.
Sādhavo Na Hi Sarvatra Candanaṃ Na Vane Vane.

There isn't a ruby in every mountain, or pearls in the head of all elephants; neither are sadhus found everywhere, nor sandal trees in every forest.

गृहीत्वा दक्षिणां विप्रास्त्यजन्ति यजमानकम् ।
प्राप्तविद्या गुरुं शिष्या दग्धारण्यं मृगास्तथा ।।

Gṛhītvā Dakṣiṇāṃ Viprāstyajanti Yajamānakam.
Prāptavidyā Guruṃ Śiṣyā Dagdhāraṇyaṃ Mṛgāstathā.

Brahmanas quit their patrons after receiving alms from them, scholars leave their teachers after being educated by them, and animals leave a burnt down forest.

को हि भार: समर्थानां किं दूरं व्यवसायिनाम् ।
को विदेश: सुविद्यानां क: पर: प्रियवादिनाम् ।।

Ko Hi Bhāraḥ Samarthānāṃ Kiṃ Dūraṃ Vyavasāyinām.
Ko Videśaḥ Suvidyānāṃ Kaḥ Paraḥ Priyavādinām.

Which work is too heavy for the strong and which place too distant for those who give effort? Which country is foreign to a man of true learning? Who can be harmful to one who speaks pleasantly?

एकेनापि सुपुत्रेण विद्यायुक्तेन साधुना ।
आह्लादितं कुलं सर्वं यथा चन्द्रेण शर्वरी ।।

Ekenāpi Suputreṇa Vidyāyuktena Sādhunā.
Āhlāditaṃ Kulaṃ Sarvaṃ Yathā Candreṇa Śarvarī.

As the night looks beautiful when the moon shines in the dark sky, so does a family delighted having even one learned and virtuous son.

किं जातैर्बहुभिः पुत्रैः शोकसन्तापकारकैः ।
वरमेकः कुलालम्बी यत्र विश्राम्यते कुलम् ।।

Kiṃ Jātairbahubhiḥ Putraiḥ Śokasantāpakārakaiḥ.
Varamekaḥ Kulālambī Yatra Viśrāmyate Kulam.

What is the point of having sons if they cause grief and exasperation? It is better to have a single son who can provide the whole family with some support and peacefulness.

एकोऽपि गुणवान्पुत्रो निर्गुणेन शतेन किम् ।
एकश्चन्द्रस्तमो हन्ति न च ताराः सहस्रशः ।।

Eko'pi Guṇavānputro Nirguṇena Śatena Kim.
Ekaścandrastamo Hanti Na Ca Tārāḥ Sahasraśaḥ.

A single son with good qualities is far better than a hundred lacking them. Like the moon dispelling darkness, which numerous stars cannot.

कुग्रामवासः कुलहीनसेवा कुभोजनं क्रोधमुखी च भार्या ।
पुत्रश्च मूर्खो विधवा च कन्या विनाग्निना षट्प्रदहन्ति कायम् ।।

Kugrāmavāsaḥ Kulahīnasevā
Kubhojanaṃ Krodhamukhī Ca Bhāryā.
Putraśca Mūrkho Vidhavā Ca Kanyā
Vināgninā Ṣaṭpradahanti Kāyam.

Residing in a small village devoid of proper living conditions, serving a person born of low family, and undernourished food can burn a man without fire.

एकाकिना तपो द्वाभ्यां पठनं गायनं त्रिभिः ।
चतुर्भिर्गमनं क्षेत्रं पञ्चभिर्बहुभी रणः ।।

Ekākinā Tapo Dvābhyāṃ Paṭhanaṃ Gāyanaṃ Tribhiḥ.
Caturbhirgamanaṃ Kṣetraṃ Pañcabhirbahubhī Raṇaḥ.

Religious austerities should be practiced in solitude, studied in twos and sung in threes. A journey should be undertaken by four people, agriculture by five and war by many together.

कः कालः कानि मित्राणि को देशः कौ व्ययागमौ ।
कश्चाहं का च मे शक्तिरिति चिन्त्यं मुहुर्मुहुः ।।

Kaḥ Kālaḥ Kāni Mitrāṇi Ko Deśaḥ Kau Vyayāgamau.
Kaścāhaṃ Kā Ca Me Śaktiriti Cintyaṃ Muhurmuhuḥ.

Repeatedly consider the following: the right time, the right friends, the right place, the right means of income, the right ways of spending, and the right person to derive power from.

यस्यार्थास्तस्य मित्राणि यस्यार्थास्तस्य बान्धवाः ।
यस्यार्थाः स पुमाँल्लोके यस्यार्थाः स च पण्डितः ।।

Yasyārthāstasya Mitrāṇi Yasyārthāstasya Bāndhavāḥ.
Yasyārthāḥ Sa Pumā~lloke Yasyārthāḥ Sa Ca Paṇḍitaḥ.

Those who have wealth possess friends. Those who are wealthy have relatives. The rich alone is deemed a man, while the affluent alone is respected as a pandit.

शकटं पञ्चहस्तेन दशहस्तेन वाजिनम् ।
गजं हस्तसहस्रेण देशत्यागेन दुर्जनम् ।।

Śakaṭaṃ Pañcahastena Daśahastena Vājinam.
Gajaṃ Hastasahasreṇa Deśatyāgena Durjanam.

Keep a thousand cubits away from an elephant, a hundred from a horse, ten from a horned beast, but keep your distance from the wicked by leaving the country.

हस्ती अङ्कुशमात्रेण वाजी हस्तेन ताड्यते ।
शृङ्गी लगुडहस्तेन खड्गहस्तेन दुर्जनः ।।

Hastī Aṅkuśamātreṇa Vājī Hastena Tāḍyate.
Śṛṅgī Laguḍahastena Khaḍgahastena Durjanaḥ.

An elephant is controlled with a goad, a horse with a slap, a horned animal with the show of a stick, and a scoundrel with a sword.

स्वर्गस्थितानामिह जीवलोके, चत्वारि चिह्नानि वसन्ति देहे।
दानप्रसंगो मधुरा च वाणी, देवार्चनं ब्राह्मणतर्पणं च।।

Svargasthitānāmiha Jīvaloke,
Catvāri Cihnāni Vasanti Dehe.
Dānaprasaṃgo Madhurā Ca Vāṇī,
Devārcanaṃ Brāhmaṇatarpaṇaṃ Ca.

The person with these four characteristics will enjoy heaven: charity, sweet words, worship of the supreme and providing the needs of the brahmanas.

परस्परस्य मर्माणि ये भाषन्ते नराधमाः ।
त एव विलयं यान्ति वल्मीकोदरसर्पवत् ॥

Parasparasya Marmāṇi Ye Bhāṣante Narādhamāḥ.
Ta Eva Vilayaṃ Yānti Valmīkodarasarpavat.

Those crooked men who speak of the hidden faults of others ultimately destroy themselves like serpents that stray onto anthills.

यस्य स्नेहो भयं तस्य स्नेहो दुःखस्य भाजनम् ।
स्नेहमूलानि दुःखानि तानि त्यक्त्वा वसेत् सुखम् ॥

Yasya Sneho Bhayaṃ Tasya Sneho Duḥkhasya Bhājanam.
Snehamūlāni Duḥkhāni Tāni Tyaktvā Vaset Sukham.

Those who are overly attached to their family experiences fear and sorrow, for the root cause of all sorrow is attachment. Thus one should shun attachments to live a peaceful life.

राज्ञि धर्मिणि धर्मिष्ठाः पापे पापाः समे समाः ।
राजानमनुवर्तन्ते यथा राजा तथा प्रजाः ॥

Rājñi Dharmiṇi Dharmiṣṭhāḥ Pāpe Pāpāḥ Same Samāḥ.
Rājānamanuvartante Yathā Rājā Tathā Prajāḥ.

If the ruler is virtuous, then the people are also virtuous. If the ruler is sinful, then the people also become sinful. If he is mediocre, then his people are mediocre. The people follow the example of the ruler. In short, as is the ruler so are the people.

पुनर्वित्तं पुनर्मित्रं पुनर्भार्या पुनर्मही ।
एतत्सर्वं पुनर्लभ्यं न शरीरं पुनः पुनः ॥

Punarvittaṃ Punarmitraṃ Punarbhāryā Punarmahī.
Etatsarvaṃ Punarlabhyaṃ Na Śarīraṃ Punaḥ Punaḥ.

An enemy can be defeated by the union of large numbers of people, just as grass through its unison wards off erosion caused by heavy rainfall.

दाने तपसि शौर्ये वा विज्ञाने विनये नये ।
विस्मयो नहि कर्तव्यो बहुरत्ना वसुन्धरा ॥

Dāne Tapasi Śaurye Vā Vijñāne Vinaye Naye.
Vismayo Nahi Kartavyo Bahuratnā Vasundharā.

Those who are actually far way may be near if they live in our mind; but he who lives not in our heart is far though he may really be nearby.

त्यजन्ति मित्राणि धनैर्विहीनं
पुत्राश्च दाराश्च सुहृज्जनाश्च ।
तमर्थवन्तं पुनराश्रयन्ति
अर्थो हि लोके मनुष्यस्य बन्धुः ॥

Tyajanti Mitrāṇi Dhanairvihīnaṃ
Putrāśca Dārāśca Suhṛjjanāśca.
Tamarthavantaṃ Punarāśrayanti
Artho Hi Loke Manuṣyasya Bandhuḥ.

He who loses his wealth is forsaken by his friends, wife, servants and relations; yet when he regains the riches, those who have forsaken him will ultimately come back to him. Hence, money is certainly the only friend in this kalyug.

पीतः क्रुद्धेन तातश्चरणतलहतो वल्लभो येन रोषा
दाबाल्याद्विप्रवर्यैः स्ववदनविवरे धार्यते वैरिणी मे ।
गेहं मे छेदयन्ति प्रतिदिवसमुमाकान्तपूजानिमित्तं
तस्मात्खिन्ना सदाहं द्विजकुलनिलयं नाथ युक्तं त्यजामि ॥

Pītaḥ Kruddhena Tātaścaraṇatalahato
Vallabho Yena Roṣā
Dābālyādvipravaryaiḥ Svavadanavivare
Dhāryate Vairiṇī Me.
Gehaṃ Me Chedayanti
Pratidivasamumākāntapūjānimittaṃ
Tasmātkhinnā Sadāhaṃ Dvijakulanilayaṃ
Nātha Yuktaṃ Tyajāmi.

Lord Vishnu asked Goddess Lakshmi, why She did not care to live in the house of a Brahmana and She replied 'O Lord, a rishi named Agastya in anger drank up My father (the ocean) and Brighu Muni kicked You; Brahmanas take pride in their learning having sought the favour of Saraswati; and lastly, each day, they pluck lotuses which is My abode, and therewith worship Lord Shiva. Therefore, O Lord, I fear to dwell with a Brahmana.'

संसारविषवृक्षस्य द्वे फलेऽमृतोपमे ।
सुभाषितं च सुस्वादु सङ्गतिः सज्जने जने ॥

Saṃsāraviṣavṛkṣasya Dve Phale'mṛtopame.
Subhāṣitaṃ Ca Susvādu Saṅgatiḥ Sajjane Jane.

There are two nectarine fruits hanging from the tree of this world; one is the hearing of sweet words such as Krishna-katha and the other, the spiritual ideas of saintly men.

◆

On Behaviour and Devotion

Chanakya enlightens people by telling them that it does not matter what our place of origin is, what our status is or if there is wealth piled up or not; whether we belong to the elite one per cent of the population or not. The only thing that matters is work, and one's dedication to it. Anything can be manifested in life if one strives relentlessly. It is work that defines our worth in this world. Success does not judge one with the possessions and class but it surely judges based on whether one deserves it or not. Chanakya says that one should not feel small in front of people who have more in any aspect of life. Most of the people in this world want to achieve things without putting in much effort and continue with their lethargy which only leads to a plain, simple and normal life. One needs to build confidence and self-worth so as to see one is truly worthy of the goal set in life. In this world where people are inclined towards superficial gains, others who do not have enough resources tend to feel intimidated and become reluctant to portray who they truly are and what they can achieve.

Being humble untangles many problems in life. It sets one free from the clutches of desire and prevents unhappiness from entering life. It also helps one develop a sense of self-control which in turn helps control anger, because that can be the reason for self destruction. Only people who do not let anger overpower their rationale can acheive peace in life. People tend to regret many actions they carried out of anger. Self-discipline not only prevents one from letting emotions drive the mind but, it also stops one from committing any mistakes which can destroy the results of one's hard work. It is this self-control that keeps pushing people towards their goals in life.

This lesson of Chanakya also gives assurance to the people in the contemporary times. Many people who have had everything in life have failed to establish their identity other than those attached to them by birth, but, on the other hand, some people rose from being nameless humans to the throne of success and inspired people with their attitude of not letting a single failure or their background to determine the extent of their success.

Chanakya is one of the few individuals in the word who has been accepted as a genius by scholars throughout the world. Reasons have been justified in every domain about his wisdom. His functional ideas are a blend of practical wisdom binded with spirituality which inspires and guides one and all to follow the path of truth. The earth is supported by the power of truth; it is the power of truth that makes the sun shine and the winds blow; indeed all things rest upon truth in his opinion.

❖

तावद्भयेषु भेतव्यं यावद्भयमनागतम् ।
आगतं तु भयं वीक्ष्य प्रहर्तव्यमशङ्कया ।।

Tāvadbhayeṣu Bhetavyaṃ Yāvadbhayamanāgatam.
Āgataṃ Tu Bhayaṃ Vīkṣya Prahartavyamaśaṅkayā.

A thing may be dreaded as long as it has not taken over one, and one should not do anything that causes that thing to overtake. However, once it has won over you, try to get rid of it without hesitation.

नात्यन्तं सरलैर्भाव्यं गत्वा पश्य वनस्थलीम् ।
छिद्यन्ते सरलास्तत्र कुब्जास्तिष्ठन्ति पादपाः ।।

Nātyantaṃ Saralairbhāvyaṃ Gatvā Paśya Vanasthalīm.
Chidyante Saralāstatra Kubjāstiṣṭhanti Pādapāḥ.

Do not be very upright in your dealings since you might observe that in a forest, straight trees are cut down first while the crooked ones are left alone.

यो ध्रुवाणि परित्यज्य अध्रुवं परिषेवते ।
ध्रुवाणि तस्य नश्यन्ति चाध्रुवं नष्टमेव हि ।।

Yo Dhruvāṇi Parityajya Adhruvaṃ Pariṣevate.
Dhruvāṇi Tasya Naśyanti Cādhruvaṃ Naṣṭameva Hi.

He who gives up what is eternal for something which is transient loses that which is eternal; and doubtlessly loses that which is transient also.

कालः पचति भूतानि कालः संहरते प्रजाः ।
कालः सुप्तेषु जागर्ति कालो हि दुरतिक्रमः ।।

Kālaḥ Pacati Bhūtāni Kālaḥ Saṃharate Prajāḥ.
Kālaḥ Supteṣu Jāgarti Kālo Hi Duratikramaḥ.

Time perfects all living beings as well as kills them; it alone is awake while others are asleep. Time is insurmountable, rest upon truth.

परोक्षे कार्यहन्तारं प्रत्यक्षे प्रियवादिनम् ।
वर्जयेत्तादृशं मित्रं विषकुम्भं पयोमुखम् ।।

Parokṣe Kāryahantāraṃ Pratyakṣe Priyavādinam.
Varjayettādṛśaṃ Mitraṃ Viṣakumbhaṃ Payomukham.

Avoid anyone who talks sweetly before you but tries to wreck you behind your back; he is like a pot of poison with milk on top.

लालनाद्बहवो दोषास्ताडने बहवो गुणाः ।
तस्मात्पुत्रं च शिष्यं च ताडयेन्न तु लालयेत् ।।

Lālanādbahavo Doṣāstāḍane Bahavo Guṇāḥ.
Tasmātputraṃ Ca Śiṣyaṃ Ca Tāḍayenna Tu Lālayet.

Many bad habits develop through overindulgence and many good ones through chastisement. Hence, reprimand your son as well as your pupil to mend their ways; never indulge them.

आचारः कुलमाख्याति देशमाख्याति भाषणम् ।
सम्भ्रमः स्नेहमाख्याति वपुराख्याति भोजनम् ।।

Ācāraḥ Kulamākhyāti Deśamākhyāti Bhāṣaṇam.
Sambhramaḥ Snehamākhyāti Vapurākhyāti Bhojanam.

A man's descent may be discerned by his conduct, his country by his pronunciation of language, his friendship by his warmth, and his capacity to eat by his body.

दुर्जनस्य च सर्पस्य वरं सर्पो न दुर्जनः ।
सर्पो दंशति काले तु दुर्जनस्तु पदे पदे ।।

Durjanasya Ca Sarpasya Varaṃ Sarpo Na Durjanaḥ.
Sarpo Daṃśati Kāle Tu Durjanastu Pade Pade.

Between a scoundrel and a serpent, the serpent is the better of the two, for it strikes only at the time it is fated to kill, while the former does it at every moment.

एकेनापि सुवृक्षेण पुष्पितेन सुगन्धिना ।
वासितं तद्वनं सर्वं सुपुत्रेण कुलं यथा ।।

Ekenāpi Suvṛkṣeṇa Puṣpitena Sugandhinā.
Vāsitaṃ Tadvanaṃ Sarvaṃ Suputreṇa Kulaṃ Yathā.

A family gains fame with the birth of a moral son, much as an entire forest is made fragrant by the presence of a tree bearing fragrant blossoms.

एकेन शुष्कवृक्षेण दह्यमानेन वह्निना ।
दह्यते तद्वनं सर्वं कुपुत्रेण कुलं यथा ।।

Ekena Śuṣkavṛkṣeṇa Dahyamānena Vahninā.
Dahyate Tadvanaṃ Sarvaṃ Kuputreṇa Kulaṃ Yathā.

A rascal son can destroy an entire family, just as a single withered, dry tree can set an entire forest on fire.

उपसर्गेऽन्यचक्रे च दुर्भिक्षे च भयावहे ।
असाधुजनसम्पर्के यः पलायेत्स जीवति ।।

Upasarge'nyacakre Ca Durbhikṣe Ca Bhayāvahe.
Asādhujanasamparke Yaḥ Palāyetsa Jīvati.

One is safe if they flee from a terrifying disaster, an invasion from another country, a dreadful famine, or the company of evil people.

धर्मार्थकाममोक्षाणां यस्यैकोऽपि न विद्यते ।
अजागलस्तनस्येव तस्य जन्म निरर्थकम् ।।

Dharmārthakāmamokṣāṇāṃ Yasyaiko'pi Na Vidyate.
Ajāgalastanasyeva Tasya Janma Nirarthakam.

He who has not acquired at least one of the following: religious merit (dharma), wealth (artha), satisfaction of desires (kama), or liberation (moksa) will repeatedly born only to die.

निःस्पृहो नाधिकारी स्यान् नाकामो मण्डनप्रियः ।
नाविदग्धः प्रियं ब्रूयात्स्पष्टवक्ता न वञ्चकः ।।

Niḥspṛho Nādhikārī Syān Nākāmo Maṇḍanapriyaḥ.
Nāvidagdhaḥ Priyaṃ Brūyātspaṣṭavaktā Na Vañcakaḥ.

If your hands are clean, you won't want to hold office; if you have no desires, you don't care about your appearance;

if you're only half educated, you can't speak nicely; and if you speak the truth, you can't be a fraud.

अभ्यासाद्धार्यते विद्या कुलं शीलेन धार्यते ।
गुणेन ज्ञायते त्वार्य: कोपो नेत्रेण गम्यते ।।

Abhyāsāddhāryate Vidyā Kulaṃ Śīlena Dhāryate.
Guṇena Jñāyate Tvāryaḥ Kopo Netreṇa Gamyate.

A respected person is identified by his exceptional qualities, knowledge is retained by practice, family pride is maintained by upholding good behaviour, and wrath is visible in the eyes.

अन्यथा वेदशास्त्राणि ज्ञानपाण्डित्यमन्यथा ।
अन्यथा तत्पदं शान्तं लोका: क्लिश्यन्ति चाह्यथा ।।

Anyathā Vedaśāstrāṇi Jñānapāṇḍityamanyathā.
Anyathā Tatpadaṃ Śāntaṃ Lokāḥ Kliśyanti Cāhnyathā.

People who mock Vedic learning, mock the sastras recommended way of living, and make fun of men with calm dispositions suffer needlessly.

दारिद्र्यनाशनं दानं शीलं दुर्गतिनाशनम् ।
अज्ञाननाशिनी प्रज्ञा भावना भयनाशिनी ।।

Dāridryanāśanaṃ Dānaṃ Śīlaṃ Durgatināśanam.
Ajñānanāśinī Prajñā Bhāvanā Bhayanāśinī.

Poverty is eradicated by charity, misery by ethical behaviour, ignorance by discretion, and fear by examination.

नास्ति कामसमो व्याधिर्नास्ति मोहसमो रिपु: ।
नास्ति कोपसमो वह्निर्नास्ति ज्ञानात्परं सुखम् ।।

Nāsti Kāmasamo Vyādhirnāsti Mohasamo Ripuḥ.
Nāsti Kopasamo Vahnirnāsti Jñānātparaṃ Sukham.

No illness is as harmful as lust, no foe like infatuation, no fire like fury, and no joy like spiritual awareness.

जन्ममृत्यू हि यात्येको भुनक्त्येकः शुभाशुभम् ।
नरकेषु पतत्येक एको याति परां गतिम् ॥

Janmamṛtyū Hi Yātyeko Bhunaktyekaḥ Śubhāśubham.
Narakeṣu Patatyeka Eko Yāti Parāṃ Gatim.

A man is born alone, dies alone, journeys to hell or the Supreme abode alone, and experiences both the good and bad effects of his karma alone.

तृणं ब्रह्मविदः स्वर्गस्तृणं शूरस्य जीवितम् ।
जिताशस्य तृणं नारी निःस्पृहस्य तृणं जगत् ॥

Tṛṇaṃ Brahmavidaḥ Svargastṛṇaṃ Śūrasya Jīvitam.
Jitāśasya Tṛṇaṃ Nārī Niḥspṛhasya Tṛṇaṃ Jagat.

Heaven is but a straw to a self-aware man, as is life to a brave man, a woman to a man who has subdued his senses, and the universe to a man who has no attachment to the world.

विद्या मित्रं प्रवासे च भार्या मित्रं गृहेषु च ।
व्याधितस्यौषधं मित्रं धर्मो मित्रं मृतस्य च ॥

Vidyā Mitraṃ Pravāse Ca Bhāryā Mitraṃ Gṛheṣu Ca.
Vyādhitasyauṣadhaṃ Mitraṃ Dharmo Mitraṃ Mṛtasya Ca.

Learning is a companion on the road, a wife in the household, medicine in sickness, and religious merit is the only companion after death.

नास्ति मेघसमं तोयं नास्ति चात्मसमं बलम् ।
नास्ति चक्षुःसमं तेजो नास्ति धान्यसमं प्रियम् ॥

Nāsti Meghasamaṃ Toyaṃ Nāsti Cātmasamaṃ Balam.

Nāsti Cakṣuḥsamaṃ Tejo Nāsti Dhānyasamaṃ Priyam.

There is no water the same as rainwater, no strength such as one's own, no light like one's own eyes, and no wealth more valuable than grain.

अधना धनमिच्छन्ति वाचं चौव चतुष्पदा: ।
मानवा: स्वर्गमिच्छन्ति मोक्षमिच्छन्ति देवता: ।।

Adhanā Dhanamicchanti Vācaṃ Caiva Catuṣpadāḥ.
Mānavāḥ Svargamicchanti Mokṣamicchanti Devatāḥ.

The poor desire wealth, animals desire the ability to speak, men desire heaven, and godly people desire liberation.

सत्येन धार्यते पृथ्वी सत्येन तपते रवि: ।
सत्येन वाति वायुश्च सर्वं सत्ये प्रतिष्ठितम् ।।

Satyena Dhāryate Pṛthvī Satyena Tapate Raviḥ.
Satyena Vāti Vāyuśca Sarvaṃ Satye Pratiṣṭhitam.

The power of truth sustains the earth; the power of truth causes the sun to shine and the winds to blow; indeed, all things are supported by truth.

चला लक्ष्मीश्चला: प्राणाश्चले जीवितमन्दिरे ।
चलाचले च संसारे धर्म एको हि निश्चल: ।।

Calā Lakṣmīścalāḥ Prāṇāścale Jivitamandire.
Calācale Ca Saṃsāre Dharma Eko Hi Niścalaḥ.

The Goddess of wealth is shaky, as is her breath. The duration of life is uncertain, as is the location of residence; however, in this inconstant world, religious merit alone is unmovable.

जनिता चोपनेता च यस्तु विद्यां प्रयच्छति ।
अन्नदाता भयत्राता पञ्चैते पितर: स्मृता: ।।

Janitā Copanetā Ca Yastu Vidyāṃ Prayacchati.
Annadātā Bhayatrātā Pañcaite Pitaraḥ Smṛtāḥ.

These are your fathers: the ones who gave you birth, braced you with sacred thread, taught you, fed you, and shielded you from dangerous situations.

श्रुत्वा धर्मं विजानाति श्रुत्वा त्यजति दुर्मतिम् ।
श्रुत्वा ज्ञानमवाप्नोति श्रुत्वा मोक्षमवाप्नुयात् ।।

Śrutvā Dharmaṃ Vijānāti Śrutvā Tyajati Durmatim.
Śrutvā Jñānamavāpnoti Śrutvā Mokṣamavāpnuyāt.

Hearing enables one to understand dharma, vanquish malignancy, gain knowledge, and achieve liberation from material bonds.

पक्षिणः काकश्चण्डालः पशूनां चौव कुक्कुरः ।
मुनीनां पापश्चण्डालः सर्वचाण्डालनिन्दकः ।।

Pakṣiṇaḥ Kākaścaṇḍālaḥ Paśūnāṃ Caiva Kukkuraḥ.
Munīnāṃ Pāpaścaṇḍālaḥ Sarvacāṇḍālanindakaḥ.

The crow is the vilest of birds, and the dog is the most vile of animals; the ascetic who sins is despicable, but he who slanders others is the worst chandala.

न पश्यति च जन्मान्धः कामान्धो नैव पश्यति ।
मदोन्मत्ता न पश्यन्ति अर्थी दोषं न पश्यति ।।

Na Paśyati Ca Janmāndhaḥ Kāmāndho Naiva Paśyati.
Madonmattā Na Paśyanti Arthī Doṣaṃ Na Paśyati.

Those born blind cannot see, and those enslaved by lust are similarly blind. Proud men see no evil, and those bent on acquiring wealth see no sin in their actions.

स्वयं कर्म करोत्यात्मा स्वयं तत्फलमश्नुते ।
स्वयं भ्रमति संसारे स्वयं तस्माद्विमुच्यते।।

Svayaṃ Karma Karotyātmā Svayaṃ Tatphalamaśnute.
Svayaṃ Bhramati Saṃsāre Svayaṃ Tasmādvimucyate.

The spirit soul follows its own path of karma and suffers the good and bad outcomes that arise. It entangles itself in samsara through its own actions and extricates itself through its own efforts.

प्रभूतं कार्यमल्पं वा यन्नरः कर्तुमिच्छति ।
सर्वारम्भेण तत्कार्यं सिंहादेकं प्रचक्षते ।।

Prabhūtaṃ Kāryamalpaṃ Vā Yannaraḥ Kartumicchati.
Sarvārambheṇa Tatkāryaṃ Siṃhādekaṃ Pracakṣate.

The one thing a man should learn from a lion is that whatever he intends to do should be done wholeheartedly and strenuously.

इन्द्रियाणि च संयम्य रागद्वेषविवर्जितः ।
समदुःखसुखः शान्तः तत्त्वज्ञः साधुरुच्यते ।।

Indriyāṇi Ca Saṃyamya Rāgadveṣavivarjitaḥ.
Samaduḥkhasukhaḥ Śāntaḥ Tattvajñaḥ Sādhurucyate.

A wise man should be able to control his senses like a crane and complete his task with proper knowledge of place, time, and ability.

प्रत्युत्थानं च युद्धं च संविभागं च बन्धुषु ।
स्वयमाक्रम्य भुक्तं च शिक्षेच्चत्वारि कुक्कुटात् ।।

Pratyutthānaṃ Ca Yuddhaṃ Ca Saṃvibhāgaṃ Ca Bandhuṣu.
Svayamākramya Bhuktaṃ Ca Śikṣeccatvāri Kukkuṭāt.

The four primary things to learn from a cock are to wake up on time, fight bravely, divide property fairly among relatives, and earn one's bread through hard work.

बह्वाशी स्वल्पसन्तुष्टः सनिद्रो लघुचेतनः ।
स्वामिभक्तश्च शूरश्च षडेते श्वानतो गुणाः ॥

Bahvāśī Svalpasantuṣṭaḥ Sanidro Laghucetanaḥ.
Svāmibhaktaśca Śūraśca Ṣaḍete Śvānato Guṇāḥ.

The four primary things to learn from a dog are contentment with almost nothing to eat despite having a large appetite, waking up instantly when needed despite being in a deep slumber, unwavering devotion to one's master, and bravery.

सुश्रान्तोऽपि वहेद्भारं शीतोष्णं न च श्यति ।
सन्तुष्टश्चरते नित्यं त्रीणि शिक्षेच्च गर्दभात् ॥

Suśrānto'pi Vahedbhāraṃ Śītoṣṇaṃ Na Ca Śyati.
Santuṣṭaścarate Nityaṃ Trīṇi Śikṣecca Gardabhāt.

Although tired, a donkey continues to carry the burden while being unconcerned about cold and heat and remaining content are the three most important lessons to be learned from a donkey.

अर्थनाशं मनस्तापं गृहे दुश्चरितानि च ।
वञ्चनं चापमानं च मतिमान्न प्रकाशयेत् ॥

Arthanāśaṃ Manastāpaṃ Gṛhe Duścaritāni Ca.
Vañcanaṃ Cāpamānaṃ Ca Matimānna Prakāśayet.

A wise man should never reveal his loss of wealth, mental anguish, his wife's misbehaviour, senseless words spoken by others, or any insult that has befallen him.

धनधान्यप्रयोगेषु विद्यासङ्ग्रहणे तथा ।

आहारे व्यवहारे च त्यक्तलज्जः सुखी भवेत् ॥

Dhanadhānyaprayogeṣu Vidyāsaṅgrahaṇe Tathā.
Āhāre Vyavahāre Ca Tyaktalajjaḥ Sukhī Bhavet.

He who overcomes his shyness in monetary transactions, knowledge acquisition, eating, and business is bound to be happy.

सन्तोषामृततृप्तानां यत्सुखं शान्तिरेव च ।
न च तद्धनलुब्धानामितश्चेतश्च धावताम् ॥

Santoṣāmṛtatṛptānāṃ Yatsukhaṃ Śāntireva Ca.
Na Ca Taddhanalubdhānāmitaścetaśca Dhāvatām.

Those who are satisfied by the nectar of spiritual tranquillity achieve happiness and peace. It cannot be attained by greedy people moving around aimlessly.

सन्तोषस्त्रिषु कर्तव्यः स्वदारे भोजने धने ।
त्रिषु चैव न कर्तव्योऽध्ययने जपदानयोः ॥

Santoṣastriṣu Kartavyaḥ Svadāre Bhojane Dhane.
Triṣu Caiva Na Kartavyo'dhyayane Japadānayoḥ.

One should be content with three things: his wife, food given by Providence, and wealth earned through hard work. However, these three things should never be considered sufficient: study, chanting the Lord's holy name, and charity.

अनुलोमेन बलिनं प्रतिलोमेन दुर्जनम् ।
आत्मतुल्यबलं शत्रुं विनयेन बलेन वा ॥

Anulomena Balinaṃ Pratilomena Durjanam.
Ātmatulyabalaṃ Śatruṃ Vinayena Balena Vā.

Conciliate a strong man through submission, a wicked man

through opposition, and a man of equal power to you through politeness or force.

अत्यन्तकोपः कटुका च वाणी
दरिद्रता च स्वजनेषु वैरम् ।
नीचप्रसंगः कुलहीनसेवा
चिह्नानि देहे नरकस्थितानाम् ।।

Atyantakopaḥ Kaṭukā Ca Vāṇī
Daridratā Ca Svajaneṣu Vairam.
Nīcaprasaṃgaḥ Kulahīnasevā
Cihnāni Dehe Narakasthitānām.

Hell's inhabitants have the following characteristics: extreme wrath, harsh speech, enmity with one's relatives, company with the base, and service to men of low birth.

शुनः पुच्छमिव व्यर्थं जीवितं विद्यया विना ।
न गुह्यगोपने शक्तं न च दंशनिवारणे ।।

Śunaḥ Pucchamiva Vyarthaṃ Jīvitaṃ Vidyayā Vinā.
Na Guhyagopane Śaktaṃ Na Ca Daṃśanivāraṇe.

An uneducated man's life is as useless as a dog's tail, which neither covers its rear end nor protects it from insect bites.

वाचां शौचं च मनसः शौचमिन्द्रियनिग्रहः ।
सर्वभूतदयाशौचमेतच्छौचं परार्थिनाम् ।।

Vācāṃ Śaucaṃ Ca Manasaḥ Śaucamindriyanigrahaḥ.
Sarvabhūtadayāśaucametacchaucaṃ Parārthinām.

One who wishes to ascend to the divine platform must have purity of speech, mind, senses, and a compassionate heart.

पुष्पे गन्धं तिले तैलं काष्ठेऽग्निं पयसि घृतम् ।
इक्षौ गुडं तथा देहे पश्यात्मानं विवेकतः ।।

Puṣpe Gandhaṃ Tile Tailaṃ Kāṣṭhe'gniṃ Payasi Ghṛtam.
Ikṣau Guḍaṃ Tathā Dehe Paśyātmānaṃ Vivekataḥ.

As you would seek fragrance in a flower, oil in a sesamum seed, fire in wood, ghee in milk, and jaggery (guda) in sugarcane, so you should seek the spirit that is in the body through discrimination.

अधमा धनमिच्छन्ति धनमानौ च मध्यमाः ।
उत्तमा मानमिच्छन्ति मानो हि महतां धनम् ॥

Adhamā Dhanamicchanti Dhanamānau Ca Madhyamāḥ.
Uttamā Mānamicchanti Māno Hi Mahatāṃ Dhanam.

Low-class men want wealth, middle-class men want both wealth and respect, and noblemen want only honour; thus, honour is a nobleman's true wealth.

वित्तं देहि गुणान्वितेषु मतिमन्नान्यत्र देहि क्वचित्
प्राप्तं वारिनिधेर्जलं घनमुखे माधुर्ययुक्तं सदा ।
जीवान्स्थावरजंगमांश्च सकलान्संजीव्य भूमण्डलं
भूयः पश्य तदेव कोटिगुणितं गच्छन्तमम्भोनिधिम् ॥

Vittaṃ Dehi Guṇānviteṣu Matimannānyatra Dehi Kvacit
Prāptaṃ Vārinidherjalaṃ Ghanamukhe Mādhuryayuktaṃ Sadā.
Jīvānsthāvarajaṃgamāṃśca Sakalānsaṃjīvya Bhūmaṇḍalaṃ
Bhūyaḥ Paśya Tadeva Koṭiguṇitaṃ Gacchantamambhonidhim.

Wise men should only give their wealth to the deserving and never to others. The water of the sea is received by the clouds and the rainwater enlivens all living beings on the earth, both movable (insects, animals, humans, etc.) and immovable (plants, trees, etc.). The water is then brought back to the ocean after its value has been multiplied a million times.

वृद्धकाले मृता भार्या बन्धुहस्तगतं धनम् ।
भोजनं च पराधीनं तिस्रः पुंसां विडम्बनाः ।।

Vṛddhakāle Mṛtā Bhāryā Bandhuhastagataṃ Dhanam.
Bhojanaṃ Ca Parādhīnaṃ Tisraḥ Puṃsāṃ Viḍambanāḥ.

A man who faces the following three situations is unlucky: the death of a spouse in old age, money going into the hands of relatives, and relying on others for food.

शान्तितुल्यं तपो नास्ति न सन्तोषात्परं सुखम् ।
अपत्यं च कलत्रं च सतां सङ्गतिरेव च ।।

Śāntitulyaṃ Tapo Nāsti Na Santoṣātparaṃ Sukham.
Apatyaṃ Ca Kalatraṃ Ca Satāṃ Saṅgatireva Ca.

There is no austerity comparable to a balanced mind, no happiness equivalent to contentment, no disease equivalent to greediness, and no virtue equivalent to mercy.

गुणो भूषयते रूपं शीलं भूषयते कुलम् ।
प्रासादशिखरस्थोऽपि काकः किं गरुडायते ।।

Guṇo Bhūṣayate Rūpaṃ Śīlaṃ Bhūṣayate Kulam.
Prāsādaśikharastho'pi Kākaḥ Kiṃ Garuḍāyate.

Moral excellence is an ornament for personal beauty, righteous behaviour is an ornament for high birth, success is an ornament for learning, and proper spending is an ornament for wealth.

निर्विषेणापि सर्पेण कर्तव्या महती फणा ।
विषमस्तु न चाप्यस्तु घटाटोपो भयङ्करः ।।

Nirviṣeṇāpi Sarpeṇa Kartavyā Mahatī Phaṇā.
Viṣamastu Na Cāpyastu Ghaṭāṭopo Bhayaṅkaraḥ.

He who cannot arouse fear through anger or bestow a favour when pleased cannot control or protect. What options does he have?

प्रातर्द्यूतप्रसङ्गेन मध्याह्ने स्त्रीप्रसङ्गगतः ।
रात्रौ चौरप्रसङ्गेन कालो गच्छन्ति धीमताम् ॥

Prātardyūtaprasaṅgena Madhyāhne Strīprasaṅgataḥ.
Rātrau Cauraprasaṅgena Kālo Gacchanti Dhīmatām.

Wise men spend their mornings talking about gambling, their afternoons talking about women's activities, and their nights talking about theft.

(The gambling alludes to King Yuddhisthira, a great devotee of Krishna. The second reference is to the glorious deeds of mother Sita, Lord Ramachandra's consort. The third reference alludes to Sri Krishna's endearing childhood exploits of stealing butter from the elderly cowherd ladies of Gokula. As a result, wise people should devote their mornings to the Mahabharata, their afternoons to the Ramayana, and their evenings to the Srimad-Bhagvatam.)

स्वहस्तग्रथिता माला स्वहस्तघृष्टचन्दनम् ।
स्वहस्तलिखितं स्तोत्रं शक्रस्यापि श्रियं हरेत् ॥

Svahastagrathitā Mālā Svahastaghṛṣṭacandanam.
Svahastalikhitaṃ Stotraṃ Śakrasyāpi Śriyaṃ Haret.

By making a garland for a Diety with one's own hands, grinding sandal paste for the Lord, and writing sacred texts—one is blessed with opulence equal to that of Indra.

दृष्टिपूतं न्यसेत्पादं वस्त्रपूतं पिबेज्जलम् ।
शास्त्रपूतं वदेद्वाक्यः मनःपूतं समाचरेत् ॥

Dṛṣṭipūtaṃ Nyasetpādaṃ Vastrapūtaṃ Pibejjalam.

Śāstrapūtaṃ Vadedvākyaḥ Manaḥpūtaṃ Samācaret.

We should carefully examine the path we take (ensuring that it is free of filth and/or living creatures); we should drink water that has been filtered (via a clean cloth); we should only speak words that have the sanction of the shastras, and we should only act in a way that has been carefully considered.

विप्रो वृक्षस्तस्य मूलं च सन्ध्या
वेदः शाखा धर्मकर्माणि पत्रम् ।
तस्मान्मूलं यत्नतो रक्षणीयं
छिन्ने मूले नैव शाखा न पत्रम् ॥

Vipro Vṛkṣastasya Mūlaṃ Ca Sandhyā
Vedaḥ Śākhā Dharmakarmāṇi Patram.
Tasmānmūlaṃ Yatnato Rakṣaṇīyaṃ
Chinne Mūle Naiva Śākhā Na Patram.

The brahmana is like a tree; his prayers are the roots, Vedic chanting is the branches, and religious acts are the leaves. As a result, efforts should be made to preserve the roots, because without the roots, there can be no branches or leaves.

एकवृक्षसमारूढा नानावर्णा विहङ्गमाः ।
प्रभाते दिक्षु दशसु यान्ति का तत्र वेदना ॥

Ekavṛkṣasamārūḍhā Nānāvarṇā Vihaṅgamāḥ.
Prabhāte Dikṣu Daśasu Yānti Kā Tatra Vedanā.

Many birds perch on a tree during the night, but in the morning they fly in all directions. Why should we bemoan that? Similarly, we should not be sad when we must part ways with our loved ones.

बुद्धिर्यस्य बलं तस्य निर्बुद्धेश्च कुतो बलम् ।
वने सिंहो यदोन्मत्तः मशकेन निपातितः ॥

Buddhiryasya Balaṃ Tasya Nirbuddheśca Kuto Balam.
Vane Siṃho Yadonmattaḥ Maśakena Nipātitaḥ.

He who has intelligence is powerful; how can a foolish man be powerful?

A small rabbit tricks the elephant of the forest, who has lost his senses due to intoxication, into falling into a lake. (This verse refers to *Panchatantra*, a famous story from the Niti-Shastra compiled by pandit Vishnusharma 2500 years ago.)

का चिन्ता मम जीवने यदि हरिर्विश्वम्भरो गीयते
नो चेदर्भकजीवनाय जननीस्तन्यं कथं निर्ममे ।
इत्यालोच्य मुहुर्मुहुर्यदुपते लक्ष्मीपते केवलं
त्वत्पादाम्बुजसेवनेन सततं कालो मया नीयते ।।

Kā Cintā Mama Jīvane Yadi Harirviśvambharo Gīyate
No Cedarbhakajīvanāya Jananīstanyaṃ Kathaṃ Nirmame.
Ityālocya Muhurmuhuryadupate Lakṣmīpate Kevalaṃ
Tvatpādāmbujasevanena Satataṃ Kālo Mayā Nīyate.

Why should I be concerned about my survival while praising Lord Vishwambhara (Vishnu), the all-powerful supporter of all? How could milk flow from a mother's breast for the nourishment of a child without the grace of Lord Hari?

दातृत्वं प्रियवक्तृत्वं धीरत्वमुचितज्ञता ।
अभ्यासेन न लभ्यन्ते चत्वार: सहजा गुणा: ।।

Dātṛtvaṃ Priyavaktṛtvaṃ Dhīratvamucitajñatā.
Abhyāsena Na Labhyante Catvāraḥ Sahajā Guṇāḥ.

Generosity, a pleasing tone, courage, and propriety of conduct are not acquired qualities, but are innate.

हस्ती स्थूलतनु: स चाङ्कुशवश: किं हस्तिमात्रोऽङ्कुशो
दीपे प्रज्वलिते प्रणश्यति तम: किं दीपमात्रं तम: ।

वज्रेणापि हताः पतन्ति गिरयः किं वज्रमात्रं नगा-
स्तेजो यस्य विराजते स बलवान्स्थूलेषु कः प्रत्ययः ॥

Hastī Sthūlatanuḥ Sa Cāṅkuśavaśaḥ Kiṃ Hastimātro'ṅkuśo
Dīpe Prajvalite Praṇaśyati Tamaḥ Kiṃ Dīpamātraṃ Tamaḥ.
Vajreṇāpi Hatāḥ Patanti Girayaḥ Kiṃ Vajramātraṃ Nagā-
Stejo Yasya Virājate Sa Balavānsthūleṣu Kaḥ Pratyayaḥ.

The elephant has a massive body but is controlled by the ankusha (goad); however, is the goad as massive as the elephant? A lit candle dispels darkness, but the candle is never as large as the darkness. A thunderbolt can break a mountain, but is the thunderbolt as big as the mountain? No, he who wields power is truly powerful; what is there in abundance?

न दुर्जनः साधुदशामुपैति
बहुप्रकारैरपि शिक्ष्यमाणः ।
आमूलसिक्तः पयसा घृतेन
न निम्बवृक्षो मधुरत्वमेति ॥

Na Durjanaḥ Sādhudaśāmupaiti
Bahuprakārairapi Śikṣyamāṇaḥ.
Āmūlasiktaḥ Payasā Ghṛtena
Na Nimbavṛkṣo Madhuratvameti.

A wicked man will not attain sanctity no matter how many times he is instructed; similarly, a neem tree will not turn sweet no matter how many times it is sprinkled with milk and ghee from the top to the roots.

अन्तर्गतमलो दुष्टस्तीर्थस्नानशतैरपि ।
न शुध्यति यथा भाण्डं सुराया दाहितं च सत् ॥

Antargatamalo Duṣṭastīrthasnānaśatairapi.
Na Śudhyati Yathā Bhāṇḍaṃ Surāyā Dāhitaṃ Ca Sat.

Similar to how a wine container cannot be purified even after all the wine has been evaporated through fire, mental dirt cannot be removed even after bathing a hundred times in the holy waters.

ये तु संवत्सरं पूर्णं नित्यं मौनेन भुञ्जते ।
युगकोटिसहस्रं तैः स्वर्गलोके महीयते ॥

Ye Tu Saṃvatsaraṃ Pūrṇaṃ Nityaṃ Maunena Bhuñjate.
Yugakoṭisahasraṃ Taiḥ Svargaloke Mahīyate.

He who can eat his meals silently (inwardly contemplating on the food) for one year attains the celestial planets for a thousand crores of years.

कामक्रोधौ तथा लोभं स्वादुशृङ्गारकौतुके ।
अतिनिद्रातिसेवे च विद्यार्थी ह्यष्ट वर्जयेत् ॥

Kāmakrodhau Tathā Lobhaṃ Svāduśṛṅgārakautuke.
Atinidrātiseve Ca Vidyārthī Hyaṣṭa Varjayet.

The following eight emotions/habits should be entirely renounced by the student (brahmachari): lust, rage, greed, desire for sweets, feeling of embellishing the body, excessive curiosity, excessive sleep, and excessive effort for bodily maintenance.

लौकिके कर्मणि रतः पशूनां परिपालकः ।
वाणिज्यकृषिकर्मा यः स विप्रो वैश्य उच्यते ॥

Laukike Karmaeed, desire for sweets,
sense of decorating the body, excessive curiosi

A vaishya is a brahmana who is involved in worldly concerns like as business, rearing animals, and farming.

लाक्षादितैलनीलीनां कौसुम्भमधुसर्पिषाम् ।

विक्रेता मद्यमांसानां स विप्रः शूद्र उच्यते ॥

Lākṣāditailanīlīnāṃ Kausumbhamadhusarpiṣām.
Vikretā Madyamāṃsānāṃ Sa Vipraḥ Śūdra Ucyate.

A shudra is a brahmana who deals in die, articles, oil, indigo, silken fabric, honey, clarified butter, liquor, or meat.

परकार्यविहन्ता च दाम्भिकः स्वार्थसाधकः ।
छली द्वेषी मृदुः क्रूरो विप्रो मार्जार उच्यते ॥

Parakāryavihantā Ca Dāmbhikaḥ Svārthasādhakaḥ.
Chalī Dveṣī Mṛduḥ Krūro Vipro Mārjāra Ucyate.

A cat-like brahmana is one who obstructs the actions of others, exhibits hypocrisy, is self-centered, harbours malice in his heart, and speaks softly while harbouring hatred.

वापीकूपतडागानामारामसुरवेश्मनाम् ।
उच्छेदने निराशङ्कः स विप्रो म्लेच्छ उच्यते ॥

Vāpīkūpataḍāgānāmārāmasuraveśmanām.
Ucchedane Nirāśaṅkaḥ Sa Vipro Mleccha Ucyate.

A mleccha is a brahmana who damages a garden, a temple, a well, a tank, or a pond.

देवद्रव्यं गुरुद्रव्यं परदाराभिमर्शनम् ।
निर्वाहः सर्वभूतेषु विप्रश्चाण्डाल उच्यते ॥

Devadravyaṃ Gurudravyaṃ Paradārābhimarśanam.
Nirvāhaḥ Sarvabhūteṣu Vipraścāṇḍāla Ucyate.

A chandala is a brahmana who cohabitates with another person's wife, steals from gurus and temple deities, and supports himself by consuming everything and everything.

देयं भोज्यधनं धनं सुकृतिभिर्नो सञ्चयस्तस्य वै

श्रीकर्णस्य बलेश्च विक्रमपतेरद्यापि कीर्तिः स्थिता ।
अस्माकं मधुदानभोगरहितं नाथं चिरात्संचितं
निर्वाणादिति नैजपादयुगलं धर्षन्त्यहो मक्षिकाः ।।

Deyaṃ Bhojyadhanaṃ Dhanaṃ Sukṛtibhirno Sañcayastasya Vai
Śrīkarṇasya Baleśca Vikramapateradyāpi Kīrtiḥ Sthitā.
Asmākaṃ Madhudānabhogarahitaṃ Nāthaṃ Cirātsaṃcitaṃ
Nirvāṇāditi Naijapādayugalaṃ Dharṣantyaho Makṣikāḥ.

The fortunate should donate all they have extra to charity. Karna, Bali, and King Vikramaditya continue to exist today thanks to generosity. They thought, 'Alas!' just by looking at the poor honeybees, flapping their legs in sorrow. 'Our honey supply had not been consumed or donated, and now it has been abruptly snatched from us by someone.'

आर्तेषु विप्रेषु दयान्वितश्च
यच्छ्रद्धया स्वल्पमुपैति दानम् ।
अनन्तपारमुपैति राजन्
यद्दीयते तन्न लभेद्द्विजेभ्यः ।।

Ārteṣu Vipreṣu Dayānvitaśca
Yacchraddhayā Svalpamupaiti Dānam.
Anantapāramupaiti Rājan
Yaddīyate Tanna Labheddvijebhyaḥ.

One who genuinely contributes even a small amount to a struggling brahmana always receives something back. As a result, whatever donated to a good brahmana will be returned to them in large quantities.

हस्तौ दानविवर्जितौ श्रुतिपुटौ सारस्वतद्रोहिणौ
नेत्रे साधुविलोकनेन रहिते पादौ न तीर्थं गतौ ।
अन्यायार्जितवित्तपूर्णमुदरं गर्वेण तुङ्ग शिरो
रे रे जम्बुक मुञ्च मुञ्च सहसा नीचं सुनिन्द्यं वपुः ।।

Hastau Dānavivarjitau Śrutipuṭau Sārasvatadrohiṇau
Netre Sādhuvilokanena Rahite Pādau Na Tīrthaṃ Gatau.
Anyāyārjitavittapūrṇamudaraṃ Garveṇa Tuṅgaṃ Śiro
Re Re Jambuka Muñca Muñca Sahasā Nīcaṃ Sunindyaṃ Vapuḥ.

O jackal, get off that man's corpse right now. His hands have never performed acts of kindness, his ears have never heard the voice of knowledge, his eyes have never seen a sincere follower of the Lord, his feet have never walked through holy places, and his head is held high in conceit. O jackal, you must not consume that or you will get contaminated.

प्रलये भिन्नमर्यादा भवन्ति किल सागराः ।
सागरा भेदमिच्छन्ति प्रलयेऽपि न साधवः ॥

Pralaye Bhinnamaryādā Bhavanti Kila Sāgarāḥ.
Sāgarā Bhedamicchanti Pralaye'pi Na Sādhavaḥ.

The seas will go beyond their capacity and seek change at the time of the pralaya (universal catastrophe), but a holy man never changes. Because of this, a saint is superior to the ocean.

उद्योगे नास्ति दारिद्यं जपतो नास्ति पातकम् ।
मौनेन कलहो नास्ति नास्ति जागरिते भयम् ॥

Udyoge Nāsti Dāridryaṃ Japato Nāsti Pātakam.
Maunena Kalaho Nāsti Nāsti Jāgarite Bhayam.

For the hard-working, poverty does not exist. A person who performs japa (chanting of the holy names of the Lord) does not acquire sin. No one disputes with those who are engrossed in maun (quiet contemplation of the Lord), and they are courageous and always vigilant.

मूर्खा यत्र न पूज्यन्ते धान्यं यत्र सुसञ्चितम् ।
दाम्पत्ये कलहो नास्ति तत्र श्रीः स्वयमागता ॥

Mūrkhā Yatra Na Pūjyante Dhānyaṃ Yatra Susañcitam.
Dāmpatye Kalaho Nāsti Tatra Śrīḥ Svayamāgatā.

Lakshmi, the goddess of fortune, appears when idiots are not taken seriously, grain is stored correctly, and husbands and wives coexist peacefully.

तादृशी जायते बुद्धिर्व्यवसायोऽपि तादृशः ।
सहायास्तादृशा एव यादृशी भवितव्यता ।।

Tādṛushī Jāyate Buddhirvyavasāyo'pi Tādṛushah.
Sahāyāstādṛushā Ev Yādṛushī Bhavitavyatā.

One's intellect operates in accordance with Providence's will; one's actions are likewise guided by fateful circumstances; and, thanks to Providence, one is surrounded by friends and family.

तुष्यन्ति भोजने विप्रा मयूरा घनगर्जिते ।
साधवः परसम्पत्तौ खलाः परविपत्तिषु ।।

Tuṣhyanti Bhojane Viprā Mayūrā Ghanagarjite.
Sādhavah Parasampattau Khalāah Paravipattiṣhu.

A satisfying dinner, a peacock in the peak of thunder, a sadhu's prosperity and the agony of others are all sources of satisfaction for Brahmanas.

नाग्निहोत्रं विना वेदा न च दानं विना क्रिया ।
न भावेन विना सिद्धिस्तस्माद्भावो हि कारणम् ।।

Nāgnihotran Vinā Vedā Na Ca Dānan Vinā Kriyā.
Na Bhāven Vinā Siddhistasmādbhāvo Hi Kāraṇam.

It is useless to recite the Vedas without offering ceremonial sacrifices to the Supreme Lord through Agni, and to offer sacrifices without also offering a contribution. However, making a donation is likewise pointless if one's thoughts are not pure at the moment.

दुर्जनं सज्जनं कर्तुमुपायो नहि भूतले ।
अपानं शातधा धौतं न श्रेष्ठमिन्द्रियं भवेत् ।।

Durjanaṃ Sajjanaṃ Kartumupāyo Nahi Bhūtale.
Apānaṃ Śātadhā Dhautaṃ Na Śreṣṭhamindriyaṃ Bhavet.

A bad guy cannot be changed by anything, just as the inferior parts of the body cannot become superior after being cleansed a hundred times.

आप्तद्वेषाद्भवेन्मृत्युः परद्वेषाद्धनक्षयः ।
राजद्वेषाद्भवेन्नाशो ब्रह्मद्वेषात्कुलक्षयः ।।

Āptadveṣhādbhavenmṛutyuah Paradveṣhāddhanakṣhayah.
Rājadveṣhādbhavennāsho Brahmadveṣhātkulakṣhayah.

Offending a kinsman results in the loss of life; offending others results in the loss of money; insulting the king results in the loss of everything; and offending a Brahmana results in the destruction of one's whole family.

सत्सङ्गाद्भवति हि साधुना खलानां
साधूनां न हि खलसंगतः खलत्वम् ।
आमोदं कुसुमभवं मृदेव धत्ते
मृद्गन्धं नहि कुसुमानि धारयन्ति ।।

Satsaṅgādbhavati Hi Sādhunā Khalānāṃ
Sādhūnāṃ Na Hi Khalasaṃgataḥ Khalatvam.
Āmodaṃ Kusumabhavaṃ Mṛdeva Dhatte
Mṛdgandhaṃ Nahi Kusumāni Dhārayanti.

In the presence of a devotee, the evil may acquire saintly traits, but the devotee does not become impious in the presence of the wicked. A flower that falls on the soil scents it, yet the flower does not take in the aroma of the earth.

साधूनां दर्शनं पुण्यं तीर्थभूता हि साधवः ।
कालेन फलते तीर्थं सद्यः साधुसमागमः ।।

Sādhūnāṃ Darśanaṃ Puṇyaṃ Tīrthabhūtā Hi Sādhavaḥ.
Kālena Phalate Tīrthaṃ Sadyaḥ Sādhusamāgamaḥ.

Meeting a devotee is a privilege because the devotee has the potential to purify immediately, whereas the sacred journey provides purity only after lengthy interaction.

विप्रास्मिन्नगरे महान्कथय कस्तालद्रुमाणां गणः
को दाता रजको ददाति वसनं प्रातर्गृहीत्वा निशि ।
को दक्षः परवित्तदारहरणे सर्वोऽपि दक्षो जनः
कस्माज्जीवसि हे सखे विषकृमिन्यायेन जीवाम्यहम् ।।

Viprāsminnagare Mahānkathaya Kastāladrumāṇāṃ Gaṇaḥ
Ko Dātā Rajako Dadāti Vasanaṃ Prātargṛhītvā Niśi.
Ko Dakṣaḥ Paravittadāraharaṇe Sarvo'pi Dakṣo Janaḥ
Kasmājjīvasi He Sakhe Viṣakṛminyāyena Jīvāmyaham.

A stranger arrives in a city and asks a brahmana, 'Who is the greatest in this city?' 'The cluster of palm trees is fantastic,' said the brahmana. The traveller then inquired, 'Who is the most benevolent person in this city?' 'The washerman who takes the garments in the morning and returns them in the evening is the most compassionate,' the Brahmana said. He then said, 'Who is the most capable guy in this city?' 'Everyone adept in stealing others of their women and fortune,' the brahmana said. 'How do you manage to survive in such a city?' the guy then questioned the brahmana. 'As a worm thrives in a dirty area, so do I!' said the brahmana.

न विप्रपादोदककर्दमाणि न वेदशास्त्रध्वनिगर्जितानि ।
स्वाहास्वधाकारविवर्जितानि श्मशानतुल्यानि गृहाणि तानि ।।

Na Viprapādodakakardamāṇi Na Vedaśāstradhvanigarjitāni.
Svāhāsvadhākāravivarjitāni Śmaśānatulyāni Gṛhāṇi Tāni.

A dwelling in which brahmanas' feet are not washed, Vedic mantras are not read aloud, and the sacred ceremonies of svaha (sacrificial sacrifices to the Supreme Lord) and swadha (offerings to the ancestors) are not conducted is analogous to a cremation.

सत्यं माता पिता ज्ञानं धर्मो भ्राता दया सखा ।
शान्तिः पत्नी क्षमा पुत्रः षडेते मम बान्धवाः ।।

Satyaṃ Mātā Pitā Jñānaṃ Dharmo Bhrātā Dayā Sakhā.
Śāntiḥ Patnī Kṣamā Putraḥ Ṣaḍete Mama Bāndhavāḥ.

When questioned about his family, a sadhu said, 'Truth is my mother, and spiritual understanding is my father; virtuous behaviour is my brother, and mercy is my friend; inner peace is my wife, and forgiveness is my son; these six are my kinsmen.'

अनित्यानि शरीराणि विभवो नैव शाश्वतः ।
नित्यं संनिहितो मृत्युः कर्तव्यो धर्मसङ्ग्रहः ।।

Anityāni Śarīrāṇi Vibhavo Naiva Śāśvataḥ.
Nityaṃ Saṃnihito Mṛtyuḥ Kartavyo Dharmasaṅgrahaḥ.

Our bodies are fleeting, riches is not eternal, and death is never far away. As a result, we must instantly engage in meritorious activities.

मातृवत्परदारेषु परद्रव्येषु लोष्ट्रवत् ।
आत्मवत्सर्वभूतेषु यः पश्यति स पण्डितः ।।

Mātṛvatparadāreṣu Paradravyeṣu Loṣṭravat.
Ātmavatsarvabhūteṣu Yaḥ Paśyati Sa Paṇḍitaḥ.

He who considers another man's wife to be his mother, riches that does not belong to him to be dirt, and the joy and agony of all other living creatures to be his own—he genuinely views things in the correct perspective, and he is a true pandit.

धर्मे तत्परता मुखे मधुरता दाने समुत्साहता
मित्रेऽवञ्चकता गुरौ विनयता चित्तेऽतिमभीरता ।
आचारे शुचिता गुणे रसिकता शास्त्रेषु विज्ञानता
रूपे सुन्दरता शिवे भजनता त्वय्यस्ति भो राघव ।।

Dharme Tatparatā Mukhe Madhuratā Dāne Samutsāhatā
Mitre'vañcakatā Gurau Vinayatā Citte'timabhīratā.
Ācāre Śucitā Guṇe Rasikatā Śāstreṣu Vijñānatā
Rūpe Sundaratā Śive Bhajanatā Tvayyasti Bho Rāghava.

'O Raghava, you have the love of virtue, pleasing speech, and an ardent desire to perform charitable acts, guileless dealings with friends, humility in the presence of the guru, deep tranquillity of mind, pure conduct, discernment of virtues, realized knowledge of the sastras, beauty of form, and devotion to God.' (At the time of Lord Ramachandra's intended coronation, the great philosopher Vasistha Muni, the spiritual teacher of the sun dynasty, stated this to Him.)

काष्ठं कल्पतरुः सुमेरुचलश्चिन्तामणिः प्रस्तरः
सूर्यास्तीव्रकरः शशी क्षयकरः क्षारो हि वारां निधिः ।
कामो नष्टतनुर्वलिर्दितिसुतो नित्यं पशुः कामगौ–
नैतांस्ते तुलयामि भो रघुपते कस्योपमा दीयते ।।

Kāṣṭhaṃ Kalpataruḥ Sumerucalaścintāmaṇiḥ Prastaraḥ
Sūryāstīvrakaraḥ Śaśī Kṣayakaraḥ Kṣāro Hi Vārāṃ Nidhiḥ.

Kāmo Naṣṭatanurvalirditisuto Nityaṃ Paśuḥ Kāmagau-
Rnaitāṃste Tulayāmi Bho Raghupate Kasyopamā Dīyate.

The wish-fulfilling jewel is merely a stone, the sun is scorching, the moon is prone to waning, the endless ocean is salty, the demigod of lust lost his body (due to Shiva's anger), Bali Maharaja, Diti's son, was born into a clan of demons, and Kamadhenu (the cow of heaven) is a mere beast. O Raghu dynasty's Lord! I cannot compare you to any of these, Lord Rama; your might far beyond theirs.

विद्या मित्रं प्रवासे च भार्या मित्रं गृहेषु च ।
व्याधितस्यौषधं मित्रं धर्मो मित्रं मृतस्य च ।।

Vidyā Mitraṃ Pravāse Ca Bhāryā Mitraṃ Gṛheṣu Ca.
Vyādhitasyauṣadhaṃ Mitraṃ Dharmo Mitraṃ Mṛtasya Ca.

Learning is our companion when we travel, the wife is our companion at home, medicine is our companion for the ill, and good actions are our companions after we pass away.

अनालोक्य व्ययं कर्ता अनाथः कलहप्रियः ।
आतुरः सर्वक्षेत्रेषु नरः शीघ्रं विनश्यति ।।

Anālokya Vyayaṃ Kartā Anāthaḥ Kalahapriyaḥ.
Āturaḥ Sarvakṣetreṣu Naraḥ Śīghraṃ Vinaśyati.

Excessive spenders, homeless urchins, quarrel mongers, and men who ignore their wives will all perish soon.

नाहारं चिन्तयेत्प्राज्ञो धर्ममेकं हि चिन्तयेत् ।
आहारो हि मनुष्याणां जन्मना सह जायते ।।

Nāhāraṃ Cintayetprājño Dharmamekaṃ Hi Cintayet.
Āhāro Hi Manuṣyāṇāṃ Janmanā Saha Jāyate.

The intelligent guy should just be concerned with practising dharma and not worry about eating. Each man's nourishment is made specifically for him from birth.

धनधान्यप्रयोगेषु विद्यासङ्ग्रहणे तथा ।
आहारे व्यवहारे च त्यक्तलज्जः सुखी भवेत् ॥

Dhanadhānyaprayogeṣu Vidyāsaṅgrahaṇe Tathā.
Āhāre Vyavahāre Ca Tyaktalajjaḥ Sukhī Bhavet.

He who is not timid in acquiring riches, wisdom, and food, as well as in having his meals, will be content.

मुहूर्तमपि जीवेच्च नरः शुक्लेन कर्मणा ।
न कल्पमपि कष्टेन लोकद्वयविरोधिना ॥

Muhūrtamapi Jīvecca Naraḥ Śuklena Karmaṇā.
Na Kalpamapi Kaṣṭena Lokadvayavirodhinā.

A man's life is honourable if he performs an auspicious deed and survives even for a brief period of time. While it is pointless to live for a kalpa (4,320,000*1000 years) if doing so just causes suffering for the two worlds (this world and the next).

गते शोको न कर्तव्यो भविष्यं नैव चिन्तयेत् ।
वर्तमानेन कालेन वर्तयन्ति विचक्षणाः ॥

Gate Śoko Na Kartavyo Bhaviṣyaṃ Naiva Cintayet.
Vartamānena Kālena Vartayanti Vicakṣaṇāḥ.

Both the past and the future shouldn't be a source of worry for us; sensible persons just focus on the present.

स्वभावेन हि तुष्यन्ति देवाः सत्पुरुषाः पिता ।
ज्ञातयः स्नानपानाभ्यां वाक्यदानेन पण्डिताः ॥

Svabhāvena Hi Tuṣyanti Devāḥ Satpuruṣāḥ Pita.
Jñātayaḥ Snānapānābhyāṃ Vākyadānena Paṇḍitāḥ.

Demigods, morally upright men, and parents are all prone to being easily delighted. When relatives are graciously welcomed with food and drink, they can be happy, and pandits can be happy to have the chance to have a spiritual discourse.

अहो बत विचित्राणि चरितानि महात्मनाम् ।
लक्ष्मीं तृणाय मन्यन्ते तद्भारेण नमन्ति च ।।

Aho Bata Vicitrāṇi Caritāni Mahātmanām.
Lakṣmīṃ Tṛṇāya Manyante Tadbhāreṇa Namanti Ca.

The actions of the powerful are peculiar; they handle riches as though it were as light as a straw, yet once they get it, they buckle under its weight.

जीवन्तं मृतवन्मन्ये देहिनं धर्मवर्जितम् ।
मृतो धर्मेण संयुक्तो दीर्घजीवी न संशयः ।।

Jīvantaṃ Mṛtavanmanye Dehinaṃ Dharmavarjitam.
Mṛto Dharmeṇa Saṃyukto Dīrghajīvī Na Saṃśayaḥ.

Even though they may be alive, those who do not live religiously are close to death, while those who pass away after living religiously continue to exist for a long time after they pass away.

धर्मार्थकाममोक्षाणां यस्यैकोऽपि न विद्यते ।
अजागलस्तनस्येव तस्य जन्म निरर्थकम् ।।

Dharmārthakāmamokṣāṇāṃ Yasyaiko'pi Na Vidyate.
Ajāgalastanasyeva Tasya Janma Nirarthakam.

One leads an absolutely pointless existence, like the nipples dangling from the neck of a goat, if he has not gained virtue, riches, pleasure, or salvation (dharma, artha, kama, moksa).

दह्यमानां सुतीव्रण नीचाः परयशोऽग्निना।
अशक्तास्तत्पदं गन्तुं ततो निन्दां प्रकुर्वते ।।

Dahyamānāṃ Sutīvraṇa Nīcāḥ Parayaśo'gninā.
Aśaktāstatpadaṃ Gantuṃ Tato Nindāṃ Prakurvate.

The fame of others ignites the hearts of evil people, and because they lack the ability to achieve such prominence themselves, they slander others.

बन्धाय विषयासङ्गो मुक्तयै निर्विषयं मनः ।
मन एव मनुष्याणां कारणं बन्धमोक्षयोः ।।

Bandhāya Viṣayāsaṅgo Muktyai Nirviṣayaṃ Manaḥ.
Mana Eva Manuṣyāṇāṃ Kāraṇaṃ Bandhamokṣayoḥ.

The mind alone is accountable for either bondage or liberation since intense attachment to sensory pleasures leads to bondage while detachment from them leads to liberty.

देहाभिमाने गलितं ज्ञानेन परमात्मनि ।
यत्र यत्र मनो याति तत्र तत्र समाधयः ।।

Dehābhimāne Galitaṃ Jñānena Paramātmani.
Yatra Yatra Mano Yāti Tatra Tatra Samādhayaḥ.

Regardless of where he be physically, he will always be engrossed in meditative trance (samadhi) if he has learned to let go of physical identity through awareness of the Supreme Self (Paramatma).

ईप्सितं मनसः सर्वं कस्य सम्पद्यते सुखम् ।
दैवायत्तं यतः सर्वं तस्मात्सन्तोषमाश्रयेत् ।।

Īpsitaṃ Manasaḥ Sarvaṃ Kasya Sampadyate Sukham.
Daivāyattaṃ Yataḥ Sarvaṃ Tasmātsantoṣamāśrayet.

Who is happy in this world to the fullest? Everything is in God's hands. As a result, contentment should be learned.

यथा धेनुसहस्रेषु वत्सो गच्छति मातरम् ।
तथा यच्च कृतं कर्म कर्तारमनुगच्छति ।।

Yathā Dhenusahasreṣu Vatso Gacchati Mātaram.
Tathā Yacca Kṛtaṃ Karma Kartāramanugacchati.

In the same way that a calf follows its mother among a thousand other cows, a man's good or bad behaviours follow him.

अनवस्थितकार्यस्य न जने न वने सुखम् ।
जनो दहति संसर्गाद्वनं संगविवर्जनात् ।।

Anavasthitakāryasya Na Jane Na Vane Sukham.
Jano Dahati Saṃsargādvanaṃ Saṃgavivarjanāt.

In the company of mankind, his heart burns from the social interaction, but in the wilderness, his helplessness burns him. A person whose acts are fragmented cannot find serenity.

कर्मायत्तं फलं पुंसां बुद्धिः कर्मानुसारिणी ।
तथापि सुधियश्चार्या सुविचार्यैव कुर्वते ।।

Karmāyattaṃ Phalaṃ Puṃsāṃ Buddhiḥ Karmānusāriṇī.
Tathāpi Sudhiyaścāryā Suvicāryaiva Kurvate.

Men get the benefits of their actions, and the actions of prior incarnations are seen in their brains. Because of this, intelligent people always proceed with caution.

एकाक्षरप्रदातारं यो गुरुं नाभिवन्दते ।
श्वानयोनिशतं गत्वा चाण्डालेष्वभिजायते ।।

Ekākṣarapradātāraṃ Yo Guruṃ Nābhivandate.
Śvānayoniśataṃ Gatvā Cāṇḍāleṣvabhijāyate.

You should honour a teacher who has taught you even one letter. The pupil who fails to do so gives birth 100 times as a dog before finally giving birth as a chandala.

जले तैलं खले गुह्यं पात्रे दानं मनागपि ।
प्राज्ञे शास्त्रं स्वयं याति विस्तारं वस्तुशक्तितः ॥

Jale Tailaṃ Khale Guhyaṃ Pātre Dānaṃ Manāgapi.
Prājñe Śāstraṃ Svayaṃ Yāti Vistāraṃ Vastuśaktitaḥ.

The secrets revealed to the wicked never remain hidden, the money given to the deserving quickly multiplies, and the knowledge provided to the deserving rapidly multiply as a tiny amount of oil is put into water.

धर्माख्याने श्मशाने च रोगिणां या मतिर्भवेत् ।
सा सर्वदैव तिष्ठेच्चेत्को न मुच्येत बन्धनात् ॥

Dharmākhyāne Śmaśāne Ca Rogiṇāṃ Yā Matirbhavet.
Sā Sarvadaiva Tiṣṭheccetko Na Mucyeta Bandhanāt.

If a man always maintains the state of mind he experiences when listening to religious teaching, being present at a cremation ground, and being unwell, how can he not get self realization?

उत्पन्नपश्चात्तापस्य बुद्धिर्भवति यादृशी ।
तादृशी यदि पूर्वं स्यात्कस्य न स्यान्महोदयः ॥

Utpannapaścāttāpasya Buddhirbhavati Yādṛśī.
Tādṛśī Yadi Pūrvaṃ Syātkasya Na Syānmahodayaḥ.

If a man should analyse before, as he does after repentance, then he would not regret his actions.

दूरस्थोऽपि न दूरस्थो यो यस्य मनसि स्थितः ।
यो यस्य हृदये नास्ति समीपस्थोऽपि दूरतः ॥

Dūrastho'pi Na Dūrastho Yo Yasya Manasi Sthitaḥ.
Yo Yasya Hṛdaye Nāsti Samīpastho'pi Dūrataḥ.

He who is in the heart may always be felt close even though he is far away. A person who is not in the heart, on the other hand, will always remain at a distance, even if he is nearby.

स जीवति गुणा यस्य यस्य धर्मः स जीवति ।
गुणधर्मविहीनस्य जीवितं निष्प्रयोजनम् ।।

Sa Jīvati Guṇā Yasya Yasya Dharmaḥ Sa Jīvati.
Guṇadharmavihīnasya Jīvitaṃ Niṣprayojanam.

He who is virtuous and pious should be regarded living, while the life of a man who is devoid of religion and virtues is devoid of any blessing.

यदीच्छसि वशीकर्तुं जगदेकेन कर्मणा ।
पुरा पञ्चदशास्येभ्यो गां चरन्ती निवारय ।।

Yadīcchasi Vaśīkartuṃ Jagadekena Karmaṇā.
Purā Pañcadaśāsyebhyo Gāṃ Carantī Nivāraya.

The following fifteen, which have a tendency to stray, should not have the upper hand over you if you want to take control of the universe by doing a single act: the five sense organs (ears, eyes, nose, tongue, and skin); the five sense objects (objects of sight, sound, smell, taste, and touch); and the five sense organs (hands, legs, mouth, genitals and anus).

तावन्मौनेन नीयन्ते कोकिलैश्चैव वासराः ।
यावत्सर्वजनानन्ददायिनी वाक्प्रवर्तते ।।

Tāvanmaunena Nīyante Kokilaiścaiva Vāsarāḥ.
Yāvatsarvajanānandadāyinī Vākpravartate.

The cuckoos are unable to sing until the spring, when they are able to make everyone happy after a protracted period of silence that spans several seasons.

धर्मं धनं च धान्यं च गुरोर्वचनमौषधम् ।
सुगृहीतं च कर्तव्यमन्यथा तु न जीवति ॥

Dharmaṃ Dhanaṃ Ca Dhānyaṃ Ca Gurorvacanamauṣadham.
Sugṛhītaṃ Ca Kartavyamanyathā Tu Na Jīvati.

The rewards for good actions, riches, crops, the teachings of the spiritual master, and rare medicines should all be protected and preserved. Without it, life would be impossible.

त्यज दुर्जनसंसर्गं भज साधुसमागमम् ।
कुरु पुण्यमहोरात्रं स्मर नित्यमनित्यतः ॥

Tyaja Durjanasaṃsargaṃ Bhaja Sādhusamāgamam.
Kuru Puṇyamahorātraṃ Smara Nityamanityataḥ.

Avoid bad company and surround yourself with good ones. Develop virtue throughout the day and night, focusing your thoughts on the everlasting while ignoring the fleeting.

युगान्ते प्रचलेन्मेरुः कल्पान्ते सप्त सागराः ।
साधवः प्रतिपन्नार्थान्न चलन्ति कदाचन ॥

Yugānte Pracalenmeruḥ Kalpānte Sapta Sāgarāḥ.
Sādhavaḥ Pratipannārthānna Calanti Kadācana.

A noble man will never be distracted, even if Sumeru Mountain were to quake at the end of a yuga or all seven oceans to be disturbed at the end of a kalpa.

यस्य चित्तं द्रवीभूतं कृपया सर्वजन्तुषु ।
तस्य ज्ञानेन मोक्षेण किं जटाभस्मलेपनैः ॥

Yasya Cittaṃ Dravībhūtaṃ Kṛpayā Sarvajantuṣu.
Tasya Jñānena Mokṣeṇa Kiṃ Jaṭābhasmalepanaiḥ.

What is the need for education, freedom, matted hair on the head, or coating the body in ashes for those whose hearts melt with love for every creature?

एकमप्यक्षरं यस्तु गुरुः शिष्यं प्रबोधयेत् ।
पृथिव्यां नास्ति तद्द्रव्यं यद्दत्त्वा सोऽनृणी भवेत् ॥

Ekamapyakṣaraṃ Yastu Guruḥ Śiṣyaṃ Prabodhayet.
Pṛthivyāṃ Nāsti Taddravyaṃ Yaddattvā So'nṛṇī Bhavet.

There is no wealth on earth that can erase the debt a student owes to his guru for having instructed him in even the smallest detail (that leads to Krishna consciousness).

कुचैलिनं दन्तमलोपधारिणं
बह्वाशिनं निष्ठुरभाषिणं च ।
सूर्योदये चास्तमिते शयानं
विमुञ्चति श्रीर्यदि चक्रपाणिः ॥

Kucailinaṃ Dantamalopadhāriṇaṃ
Bahvāśinaṃ Niṣṭhurabhāṣiṇaṃ Ca.
Sūryodaye Cāstamite Śayānaṃ
Vimuñcati Śrīryadi Cakrapāṇiḥ.

Even if a person has a lovely personality, Lakshmi won't like them if they have bad teeth, unclean clothes, are gluttons, speak harshly, or sleep beyond daybreak.

अन्यायोपार्जितं द्रव्यं दश वर्षाणि तिष्ठति ।
प्राप्ते चैकादशे वर्षे समूलं तद्विनश्यति ॥

Anyāyopārjitaṃ Dravyaṃ Daśa Varṣāṇi Tiṣṭhati.
Prāpte Caikādaśe Varṣe Samūlaṃ Tadvinaśyati.

Sinfully gained money may stay with a person for 10 years, but after that, it will dissapear with even the initial stock.

अयुक्तं स्वामिनो युक्तं युक्तं नीचस्य दूषणम् ।
अमृतं राहवे मृत्युर्विषं शङ्करभूषणम् ।।

Ayuktaṃ Svāmino Yuktaṃ Yuktaṃ Nīcasya Dūṣaṇam.
Amṛtaṃ Rāhave Mṛtyurviṣaṃ Śaṅkarabhūṣaṇam.

A good activity carried out by a low-class man ends up being condemned because no one respects him, whereas a poor act carried out by a great man is not condemned since no one can criticize him. The consumption of poison is terrible, yet when Lord Shiva drank it, transforming into a pendant for his neck. The consumption of nectar is great, but it led to Rahu's destruction.

तद्भोजनं यद्द्विजभुक्तशेषं
तत्सौहृदं यत्क्रियते परस्मिन् ।
सा प्राज्ञता या न करोति पापं
दम्भं विना यः क्रियते स धर्मः ।।

Tadbhojanaṃ Yaddvijabhuktaśeṣaṃ
Tatsauhṛdaṃ Yatkriyate Parasmin.
Sā Prājñatā Yā Na Karoti Pāpaṃ
Dambhaṃ Vinā Yaḥ Kriyate Sa Dharmaḥ.

The leftovers from a brahmana's supper are considered to be a true meal, just as true love is demonstrated for others rather than for oneself. True knowledge and an unostentatious act of charity both consist in abstaining from sin.

मणिर्लुण्ठति पादाग्रे काचः शिरसि धार्यते ।
क्रयविक्रयवेलायां काचः काचो मणिर्मणिः ।।

Maṇirluṇṭhati Pādāgre Kācaḥ Śirasi Dhāryate.
Krayavikrayavelāyāṃ Kācaḥ Kāco Maṇirmaṇiḥ.

Men's feet are covered in dust with the most priceless gems, while their heads are adorned with pieces of glass. However, we shouldn't assert that as a result, the worth of the gems has decreased while the significance of the glass fragments has increased. Each will be placed in its proper position when a person of critical judgement appears.

अनन्तशास्त्रं बहुलाश्च विद्या:
स्वल्पश्च कालो बहुविघ्नता च ।
यत्सारभूतं तदुपासनीयां
हंसो यथा क्षीरमिवाम्बुमध्यात् ।।

Anantaśāstraṃ Bahulāśca Vidyāḥ
Svalpaśca Kālo Bahuvighnatā Ca.
Yatsārabhūtaṃ Tadupāsanīyāṃ
Haṃso Yathā Kṣīramivāmbumadhyāt.

Shastric knowledge is limitless, and there are many arts to study; yet, we have a certain amount of time, and our learning possibilities are filled with difficulties. As the swan just consumes the milk in the water, choose the teachings that are most significant.

दूरागतं पथि श्रान्तं वृथा च गृहमागतम् ।
अनर्चयित्वा यो भुङ्क्ते स वै चाण्डाल उच्यते ।।

Dūrāgataṃ Pathi Śrāntaṃ Vṛthā Ca Gṛhamāgatam.
Anarcayitvā Yo Bhuṅkte Sa Vai Cāṇḍāla Ucyate.

He is a chandala who, having travelled a great distance and being extremely exhausted, eats a meal without entertaining the visitor who has come to his home.

पठन्ति चतुरो वेदान्धर्मशास्त्राण्यनेकशः ।
आत्मानं नैव जानन्ति दर्वी पाकरसं यथा ।।

Paṭhanti Caturo Vedāndharmaśāstrāṇyanekaśaḥ.
Ātmānaṃ Naiva Jānanti Darvī Pākarasaṃ Yathā.

One may be familiar with the dharma-shastras and the four Vedas, but if they lack knowledge of their own spiritual selves, they are comparable to a ladle that stirs a variety of meals but has no taste for any of them.

धन्या द्विजमयी नौका विपरीता भवार्णवे ।
तरन्त्यधोगताः सर्वे उपरिष्ठाः पतन्त्यधः ।।

Dhanyā Dvijamayī Naukā Viparītā Bhavārṇave.
Tarantyadhogatāḥ Sarve Upariṣṭhāḥ Patantyadhaḥ.

Those souls who find refuge under a real brahmana, who is comparable to a boat while navigating the ocean of life, are unquestionably blessed. They are not like the passengers on a regular ship, which is vulnerable to sinking.

अयममृतनिधानं नायकोऽप्योषधीनाम्
अमृतमयशरीरः कान्तियुक्तोऽपि चन्द्रः ।
भवतिविगतरश्मिर्मण्डलं प्राप्य भानोः
परसदननिविष्टः को लघुत्वं न याति ।।

Ayamamṛtanidhānaṃ Nāyako'pyoṣadhīnām
Amṛtamayaśarīraḥ Kāntiyukto'pi Candraḥ.
Bhavativigataraśmirmaṇḍalaṃ Prāpya Bhānoḥ
Parasadananiviṣṭaḥ Ko Laghutvaṃ Na Yāti.

Although everlasting like Amrta and beautiful in appearance, the moon is the home of nectar and the presiding deity of all medicines. When the sun rises, the moon's beams lose their brightness. Therefore, moving in with someone else's family won't make the average male feel inferior.

अलिरयं नलिनीदलमध्यगः
कमलिनीमकरन्दमदालसः ।
विधिवशात्परदेशमुपागतः
कुटजपुष्परसं बहु मन्यते ॥

Alirayaṃ Nalinīdalamadhyagaḥ
Kamalinīmakarandamadālasaḥ.
Vidhivaśātparadeśamupāgataḥ
Kuṭajapuṣparasaṃ Bahu Manyate.

The humble bee is currently eating on the ordinary kutaja flower. It usually lives amid the delicate lotus petals and sips copiously of the delicious nectar. It thinks the pollen of the kutaja is wonderful because it is in a foreign land where there are no lotuses.

बन्धनानि खलु सन्ति बहूनि
प्रेमरज्जुकृतबन्धनमन्यत् ।
दारुभेदनिपुणोऽपि षडंघ्रि-
र्निष्क्रियो भवति पंकजकोशे: ॥

Bandhanāni Khalu Santi Bahūni
Premarajjukṛtabandhanamanyat.
Dārubhedanipuṇo'pi Ṣaḍaṃghri-
Rniṣkriyo Bhavati Paṃkajakośeḥ.

The link of affection is the strongest of all the ties that may bind one and allow them to be influenced and controlled in this world. For instance, the bee gets stuck in the embrace of its favourite blossoms while being skilled in piercing tough wood (as the petals close at dusk).

छिन्नोऽपि चन्दनतरुर्न जहाति गन्धं
वृद्धोऽपि वारणपतिर्न जहाति लीलाम् ।
यन्त्रार्पितो मधुरतां न जहाति चेक्षुः
क्षीणोऽपि न त्यजति शीलगुणान्कुलीनः ॥

Chinno'pi Candanatarurna Jahāti Gandhaṃ
Vṛddho'pi Vāraṇapatirna Jahāti Līlām.
Yantrārpito Madhuratāṃ Na Jahāti Cekṣuḥ
Kṣīṇo'pi Na Tyajati Śīlaguṇānkulīnaḥ.

Even if sandalwood is chopped, it retains the authenticity of its scent, much as an elephant probably doesn't give up being active as he ages. The sugarcane retains its sweetness even after being pressed in a mill; similarly, a man of aristocratic descent should retain his high traits despite his extreme poverty.

कोऽर्थान्प्राप्य न गर्वितो विषयिणः कस्यापदोऽस्तं गताः
स्त्रीभिः कस्य न खण्डितं भुवि मनः को नाम राजप्रियः ।
कः कालस्य न गोचरत्वमगमत् कोऽर्थी गतो गौरवं
को वा दुर्जनदुर्गमेषु पतितः क्षेमेण यातः पथि ॥

Ko'rthānprāpya Na Garvito Viṣayiṇaḥ Kasyāpado'staṃ Gatāḥ
Strībhiḥ Kasya Na Khaṇḍitaṃ Bhuvi Manaḥ Ko Nāma Rājapriyaḥ.
Kaḥ Kālasya Na Gocaratvamagamat Ko'rthī Gato Gauravaṃ
Ko Vā Durjanadurgameṣu Patitaḥ Kṣemeṇa Yātaḥ Pathi.

Who is there who has not become proud after becoming wealthy? Who among the licentious has managed to put an end to his disasters? Which man in this world has not been overcome by a woman? Who has the king's undying affection? Who among us has not succumbed to the effects of time? Exactly which beggar has achieved fame? Who has gained happiness by adopting the vices of the evil?

गुणाः सर्वत्र पूज्यन्ते न महत्योऽपि सम्पदः ।
पूर्णेन्दुः किं तथा वन्द्यो निष्कलङ्को यथा कृशः ।।

Guṇāḥ Sarvatra Pūjyante Na Mahatyo'pi Sampadaḥ.
Pūrṇenduḥ Kiṃ Tathā Vandyo Niṣkalaṅko Yathā Kṛśaḥ.

Even though a guy has less money, he is still respected in society if he is moral. The Moon of Douj is adored because it is clear and has no stains at all, unlike the full moon, which is not worshipped although shining brightly.

परैरुक्तगुणो यस्तु निर्गुणोऽपि गुणी भवेत् ।
इन्द्रोऽपि लघुतां याति स्वयं प्रख्यापितैर्गुणैः ।।

Parairuktaguṇo Yastu Nirguṇo'pi Guṇī Bhavet.
Indro'pi Laghutāṃ Yāti Svayaṃ Prakhyāpitairguṇaiḥ.

Even if a person may actually be devoid of any merit, he is nonetheless acclaimed as worthy when he is seen as great by others. Even if he could be Indra, a person who shouts his own praises degrades himself in the eyes of others (the possessor of all excellences).

विवेकिनमनुप्राप्ता गुणा यान्ति मनोज्ञताम् ।
सुतरां रत्नमाभाति चामीकरनियोजितम् ।।

Vivekinamanuprāptā Guṇā Yānti Manojñatām.
Sutarāṃ Ratnamābhāti Cāmīkaraniyojitam.

If a man of discrimination has good traits, his brightness would be recognized as a stone that would unavoidably shine when set in a piece of gold jewellery.

गुणैः सर्वज्ञतुल्योऽपि सीदत्येको निराश्रयः ।
अनर्घ्यमपि माणिक्यं हेमाश्रयमपेक्षते ।।

Guṇaiḥ Sarvajñatulyo'pi Sīdatyeko Nirāśrayaḥ.

Anarghyamapi Māṇikyaṃ Hemāśrayamapekṣate.

Even someone with admirable attributes suffers without patronage; similarly, a gem, although being valuable, needs a gold setting to shine brilliantly.

अतिक्लेशेन यद्द्रव्यमतिलोभेन यत्सुखम् ।
शत्रूणां प्रणिपातेन ते ह्यर्था मा भवन्तु मे ।।

Atikleśena Yaddravyamatilobhena Yatsukham.
Śatrūṇāṃ Praṇipātena Te Hyarthā Mā Bhavantu Me.

I don't need riches that must be obtained via going through suffering, breaking moral laws, or pleading for money in front of an adversary.

किं तया क्रियते लक्ष्म्या या वधूरिव केवला ।
या तु वेश्येव सामान्या पथिकैरपि भुज्यते ।।

Kiṃ Tayā Kriyate Lakṣmyā Yā Vadhūriva Kevalā.
Yā Tu Veśyeva Sāmānyā Pathikairapi Bhujyate.

Money that is locked up in a safe serves no purpose. Similar to how a fool's riches is utilized by the dishonest and the evil, it will not assist our community.

धनेषु जीवितव्येषु स्त्रीषु चाहारकर्मसु ।
अतृप्ताः प्राणिनः सर्वे याता यास्यन्ति यान्ति च ।।

Dhaneṣu Jīvitavyeṣu Strīṣu Cāhārakarmasu.
Atṛptāḥ Prāṇinaḥ Sarve Yātā Yāsyanti Yānti Ca.

In this world, everyone who was not content to enjoy their money, food, and women has died; currently, there are others who have done the same and are also dying; and in the future, there will be others who will also die without feeling fulfilled. These desires never leave anyone satisfied; the more one indulges, the more one craves.

प्रियवाक्यप्रदानेन सर्वे तुष्यन्ति जन्तवः ।
तस्मात्तदेव वक्तव्यं वचने का दरिद्रता ।।

Priyavākyapradānena Sarve Tuṣyanti Jantavaḥ.
Tasmāttadeva Vaktavyaṃ Vacane Kā Daridratā.

All sacrifices and charitable deeds (done for material gain) will yield only transient consequences; nevertheless, gifts given to deserving individuals who are cognizant and have a conscience, as well as protection extended to all living things, will never perish.

क्षीयन्ते सर्वदानानि यज्ञहोमबलिक्रियाः ।
न क्षीयते पात्रदानमभयं सर्वदेहिनाम् ।।

Kṣīyante Sarvadānāni Yajñahomabalikriyāḥ.
Na Kṣīyate Pātradānamabhayaṃ Sarvadehinām.

It is inevitable that the qualities acquired via various types of donating, sacrificial ceremonies, fire sacrifices, oblations, and other forms of worship would deteriorate with time. But the goodness gained by giving someone in need a sense of security or protection never fades.

तृणं लघु तृणात्तूलं तूलादपि च याचकः ।
वायुना किं न नीतोऽसौ मामयं याचयिष्यति ।।

Tṛṇaṃ Laghu Tṛṇāttūlaṃ Tūlādapi Ca Yācakaḥ.
Vāyunā Kiṃ Na Nīto'sau Māmayaṃ Yācayiṣyati.

Cotton and a blade of grass are both light, but a beggar is incomparably lighter. Why then does he not get carried away by the wind? Because it is afraid of asking him for handouts.

वरं प्राणपरित्यागो मानभङ्गेन जीवनात् ।
प्राणत्यागे क्षणं दुःखं मानभङ्गे दिने दिने ।।

Varaṃ Prāṇaparityāgo Mānabhaṅgena Jīvanāt.
Prāṇatyāge Kṣaṇaṃ Duḥkhaṃ Mānabhaṅge Dine Dine.

Since there is no shortage of good words, we should speak to people in a way that is agreeable because all animals in the world like hearing them.

कृते प्रतिकृतिं कुर्याद्धिंसने प्रतिहिंसनम् ।
तत्र दोषो न पतति दुष्टे दुष्टं समाचरेत् ।।

Kṛte Pratikṛtiṃ Kuryāddhiṃsane Pratihiṃsanam.
Tatra Doṣo Na Patati Duṣṭe Duṣṭaṃ Samācaret.

A wicked person must be paid by his own resources, therefore we should return favours done to us by others by deeds of kindness as well as pay bad for evil when there is no guilt involved.

यद्दूरं यद्दुराराध्यं यच्च दूरे व्यवस्थितम् ।
तत्सर्वं तपसा साध्यं तपो हि दुरतिक्रमम् ।।

Yaddūraṃ Yaddurārādhyaṃ Yacca Dūre Vyavasthitam.
Tatsarvaṃ Tapasā Sādhyaṃ Tapo Hi Duratikramam.

Tapasya makes it simple to achieve things that are far away, seem difficult, or are out of our grasp. Absolute religious austerity is unmatched.

लोभश्चेदगुणेन किं पिशुनता यद्यस्ति किं पातकैः
सत्यं चेत्तपसा च किं शुचि मनो यद्यस्ति तीर्थेन किम्।
सौजन्यं यदि किं गुणैः सुमहिमा यद्यस्ति किं मण्डनैः
सद्विद्या यदि किं धनैरपयशो यद्यस्ति किं मृत्युना ।।

Lobhaścedaguṇena Kiṃ Piśunatā Yadyasti Kiṃ Pātakaiḥ

Satyaṃ Cettapasā Ca Kiṃ Śuci Mano Yadyasti Tīrthena Kim.
Saujanyaṃ Yadi Kiṃ Guṇaiḥ Sumahimā Yadyasti Kiṃ Maṇḍanaiḥ
Sadvidyā Yadi Kiṃ Dhanairapayaśo Yadyasti Kiṃ Mṛtyunā.

What sin is more detrimental than covetousness? What vice is worse than slander? Is there any need for austerity for the truthful? What use does a pilgrimage serve for someone with a pure heart? Is there any other virtue required if one has a nice disposition? What are other ornaments worth if a man is famous? What need does a man with practical knowledge have for wealth? And what could be worse in death for a man who has been dishonoured?

पिता रत्नाकरो यस्य लक्ष्मीर्यस्य सहोदरा ।
शङ्खो भिक्षाटनं कुर्यान्न दत्तमुपतिष्ठते ॥

Pitā Ratnākaro Yasya Lakṣmīryasya Sahodarā.
Śaṅkho Bhikṣāṭanaṃ Kuryānna Dattamupatiṣṭhate.

Even though Lakshmi, the goddess of luck, is the sister of the conch shell and the sea, the repository of all the gems, is its father, the conch still needs to knock on doors to collect alms. Therefore, it is true that nothing can be gained without first having given.

तक्षकस्य विषं दन्ते मक्षिकायास्तु मस्तके ।
वृश्चिकस्य विषं पुच्छे सर्वाङ्गे दुर्जने विषम् ॥

Takṣakasya Viṣaṃ Dante Makṣikāyāstu Mastake.
Vṛścikasya Viṣaṃ Pucche Sarvāṅge Durjane Viṣam.

The fang of a snake, the mouth of a fly, and the sting of a scorpion all contain poison, but a wicked man is full with it.

परोपकरणं येषां जागर्ति हृदये सताम् ।

नश्यन्ति विपदस्तेषां सम्पदः स्युः पदे पदे ॥

Paropakaraṇaṃ Yeṣāṃ Jāgarti Hṛdaye Satām.
Naśyanti Vipadasteṣāṃ Sampadaḥ Syuḥ Pade Pade.

The individual who cultivates compassion for all living things in his heart will eventually conquer all obstacles and be the beneficiary of many riches at every stage of life.

जन्म जन्म यदभ्यस्तं दानमध्ययनं तपः ।
तेनैवाभ्यासयोगेन देही चाभ्यस्यते पुनः ॥

Janma Janma Yadabhyastaṃ Dānamadhyayanaṃ Tapaḥ
Tenaivābhyāsayogena Dehī Cābhyasyate Punaḥ

By connecting (through yoga) this current incarnation to the previous ones, the habits of generosity, learning and austerity that were practised in earlier lifetimes continue to be fostered in this birth.

दानार्थिनो मधुकरा यदि कर्णतालैर्दूरीकृताः
दूरीकृताः करिवरेण मदान्धबुद्ध्या ।
तस्यैव गण्डयुग्ममण्डनहानिरेषा
भृंगाः पुनर्विकचपद्मवने वसन्ति ॥

Dānārthino Madhukarā Yadi Karṇatālairdūrīkṛtāḥ
Dūrīkṛtāḥ Karivareṇa Madāndhabuddhyā.
Tasyaiva Gaṇḍayugmamaṇḍanahānireṣā
Bhṛṃgāḥ Punarvikacapadmavane Vasanti.

If a lust-intoxicated elephant's flapping ears chase away bees trying to collect the liquid leaking from his head, the elephant is the one who has lost the ornament on his head. In the lake loaded with lotus, the bees are content.

◆

On Education and Fate

Chanakya emphasizes the need for education in life. He says that whatever one has acquired through education will be the only possession that will stay throughout life. The beauty will eventually fade away, youth will gradually be lost, friends will part but, education will stay forever and help in times of adversity.

The serenity of a wise mind, as well as a sense of fulfilment in life even when one is alone, are all benefits of education. A person who is not educated will not be respected by society. It also serves as a guide when no one is present. It ought to be viewed as a long-term investment that pays out in the long run. Today, education is no longer just an option; it has evolved into a social requirement and a basic human right. Institutions exist to educate even the poor. It is one of the factors that determines whether a nation is developing and thriving or not.

Acharya claims that whatever is written in destiny will happen. 'Happening cannot be avoided. It just keeps happening. At the time of being, the same favorable environment is created, our intellect also starts working accordingly.'

This statement refers to the inevitable reality that whatever is written in life, will occur. Even if one makes every effort to change or stop it, the fate that has been written is irrevocable. It happens in life that even if people want, they can not stop things from happening. These can be related with the professional, private, or any other domain which affects one directly and/or indirectly. However, hampering these estrangements will invariably lead to failure.

❖

श्लोकेन वा तदर्धेन तदर्धार्धाक्षरेण वा ।
अबन्ध्यं दिवसं कुर्याद्दानाध्ययनकर्मभिः ॥

Ślokena Vā Tadardhena Tadardhārdhākṣareṇa Vā.
Abandhyaṃ Divasaṃ Kuryāddānādhyayanakarmabhiḥ.

Don't allow a day go by without you memorising even one letter of a verse, or without engaging in charitable giving, academic pursuits, or other acts of piety.

कामधेनुगुणा विद्या ह्यकाले फलदायिनी ।
प्रवासे मातृसदृशी विद्या गुप्तं धनं स्मृतम् ॥

Kāmadhenuguṇā Vidyā Hyakāle Phaladāyinī.
Pravāse Mātṛsadṛśī Vidyā Guptaṃ Dhanaṃ Smṛtam.

Learning is similar to a kamdhenu. It always gives, just like she does. It provides for you on your journey like a mother. As a result, learning is a secret gem.

रूपयौवनसम्पन्ना विशालकुलसम्भवाः ।
विद्याहीना न शोभन्ते निर्गन्धाः किंशुका यथा ॥

Rupayuvanasampanna Vishalkulasambhava.
Vidyahina Na Shobhante Nirgandha: Kinshuka Yatha.

Men may have been born into aristocratic houses, have been gifted with beauty and youth, but without education, they are like the palasa flower, which lacks a lovely scent.

किं कुलेन विशालेन विद्याहीनेन देहिनाम् ।
दुष्कुलं चापि विदुषो देवैरपि स पूज्यते ॥

Ki Kulen Vishalen Vidyaheenen Dehinam.
Duskulam Chapi Vidusho Devairpi Sa Pujyate.

What use is a high birth if one has access to education? If a man of poor origin is erudite, even the gods will honour him.

विद्वान्प्रशस्यते लोके विद्वान् सर्वत्र पूज्यते ।
विद्यया लभते सर्वं विद्या सर्वत्र पूज्यते ।।

Vidyaanprashasyate Loke Vidyan Sarvatra Pujyate.
Vidya Labhte Sarvam Vidya Sarvatra Pujyate.

A learned man is recognized by the people. A man with wisdom is respected everywhere because of his knowledge. In fact, education is valued worldwide.

धनहीनो न हीनश्च धनिकः स सुनिश्चयः ।
विद्यारत्नेन हीनो यः स हीनः सर्ववस्तुषु ।।

Dhanahino Na Hinashch Dhanikah Sa Sunishrachayah.
Vidyaratnen Heeno Yah Sa Heenah Sarvavastushu.

If a person is educated, even when he lacks material riches, he is still wealthy; nevertheless, a person who lacks education is completely poor.

सुखार्थी चेत्त्यजेद्विद्यां विद्यार्थी चेत्त्यजेत्सुखम् ।
सुखार्थिनः कुतो विद्या सुखं विद्यार्थिनः कुतः ।।

Sukhārthī Cettyajedvidyāṃ Vidyārthī Cettyajetsukham.
Sukhārthinaḥ Kuto Vidyā Sukhaṃ Vidyārthinaḥ Kutaḥ.

One who wants knowledge must not aspire for sense gratification; one who seeks sense gratification must abandon all aspirations of learning. How does someone who wants to satisfy their senses learn, and how does someone who is already knowledgeable learn to satisfy their senses?

येषां न विद्या न तपो न दानं
ज्ञानं न शीलां न गुणो न धर्मः ।
ते मर्त्यलोके भुवि भारभूता

मनुष्यरूपेण मृगाश्चरन्ति ॥

Yeṣāṃ Na Vidyā Na Tapo Na Dānaṃ
Jñānaṃ Na Śīlāṃ Na Guṇo Na Dharmaḥ.
Te Martyaloke Bhuvi Bhārabhūtā
Manuṣyarūpeṇa Mṛgāścaranti.

Lacking in education, repentance, knowledge, a positive outlook, virtue, and charity, these people are simply brutes roaming the planet in the shape of humans. They weigh down the planet.

अन्तःसारविहीनानामुपदेशो न जायते ।
मलयाचलसंसर्गान्न वेणुश्चन्दनायते ॥

Antah Saarviheenanamupade Sho Na Jayate
Malyachalsansarganan Venushchandanayate

Just like bamboo won't turn into sandalwood by being put on the Malaya Mountain, those who are incapable of observation cannot gain from teaching.

येषां श्रीमद्यशोदासुतपदकमले नास्ति भक्तिर्नराणां
येषामाभीरकन्याप्रियगुणकथने नानुरक्ता रसज्ञा ।
येषां श्रीकृष्णलीलाललितरसकथासादरौ नैव कर्णौ
धिक् तान् धिक् तान् धिगेतान् कथयति सततं कीर्तनस्थो मृदंगः ॥

Yeṣāṃ Śrīmadyaśodāsutapadakamale Nāsti Bhaktirnarāṇāṃ
Yeṣāmābhīrakanyāpriyaguṇakathane Nānuraktā Rasajñā.
Yeṣāṃ Śrīkṛṣṇalīlālalitarasakathāsādarau Naiva Karṇau
Dhik Tān Dhik Tān Dhigetān Kathayati Satataṃ
Kīrtanastho Mṛdaṃgaḥ.

'Shame on people who don't have any love for the lotus feet of Sri Krishna, the son of mother Yashoda, who don't care about Srimati Radharani's virtues, and who aren't willing to hear the Lord's Lila stories.' In kirtana, the mrdanga sound of dhik-tam dhik-tam dhigatam is exclaimed in this manner.

पुत्राश्च विविधैः शीलैर्नियोज्याः सततं बुधैः ।
नीतिज्ञाः शीलसम्पन्ना भवन्ति कुलपूजिताः ॥

Putrāśca Vividhaiḥ Śīlairniyojyāḥ Satataṃ Budhaiḥ.
Nītijñāḥ Śīlasampannā Bhavanti Kulapūjitāḥ.

Since boys raised by wise men are well-behaved and so become a source of pride for their families, wise men should constantly take care to instil moral values in their offspring.

माता शत्रुः पिता वैरी याभ्यां बाला न पाठिताः ।
सभामध्ये न शोभन्ते हंसमध्ये बको यथा ॥

Mātā Śatruḥ Pitā Vairī Yābhyāṃ Bālā Na Pāṭhitāḥ.
Sabhāmadhye Na Śobhante Haṃsamadhye Bako Yathā.

As a crane is amid swans, so are uneducated sons in a public assembly, so are parents who do not teach their boys their enemies.

अग्निर्देवो द्विजातीनां मुनीनां हृदि दैवतम् ।
प्रतिमा स्वल्पबुद्धीनां सर्वत्र समदर्शिनः ॥

Agnirdevo Dvijātīnāṃ Munīnāṃ Hṛdi Daivatam.
Pratimā Svalpabuddhīnāṃ Sarvatra Samadarśinaḥ.

For those who were born twice, fire (Agni) stands in for God. In the hearts of His followers, the Supreme Lord resides. The Supreme Lord is everywhere, but individuals with average intelligence can only perceive Him in His srimurti.

एकोदरसमुद्भूता एकनक्षत्रजातकाः ।
न भवन्ति समाः शीले यथा बदरकण्टकाः ॥

Ekodarasamudbhūtā Ekanakṣatrajātakāḥ.
Na Bhavanti Samāḥ Śīle Yathā Badarakaṇṭakāḥ.

Even if two persons share the same womb and are born under the same stars, they would never have the same temperament as the badari tree's thousand fruits.

दूतो न सञ्चरति खे न चलेच्च वार्ता
पूर्वं न जल्पितमिदं न च सङ्गमोऽस्ति ।
व्योम्नि स्थितं रविशाशिग्रहणं प्रशस्तं
जानाति यो द्विजवरः स कथं न विद्वान् ।।

Dūto Na Sañcarati Khe Na Calecca Vārtā
Pūrvaṃ Na Jalpitamidaṃ Na Ca Saṅgamo'sti.
Vyomni Sthitaṃ Raviśāśigrahaṇaṃ Praśastaṃ
Jānāti Yo Dvijavaraḥ Sa Kathaṃ Na Vidvān.

No messenger can travel in the sky and no information comes from there either. Its occupants' voices are never heard, and no communication can be made with them. Consequently, the brahmana who foretells the solar and lunar eclipses that take place in the sky must be regarded as a man of profound intelligence.

रङ्कं करोति राजानं राजानं रङ्कमेव च ।
धनिनं निर्धनं चौव निर्धनं धनिनं विधिः ।।

Raṅkaṃ Karoti Rājānaṃ Rājānaṃ Raṅkameva Ca.
Dhaninaṃ Nirdhanaṃ Caiva Nirdhanaṃ Dhaninaṃ Vidhiḥ.

Fate turns a beggar into a king and a king into a beggar. It can make a rich man poor and a poor man rich.

पत्रं नैव यदा करीलविटपे दोषो वसन्तस्य किं
नोलूकोऽप्यवलोकते यदि दिवा सूर्यस्य किं दूषणम् ।
वर्षा नैव पतन्ति चातकमुखे मेघस्य किं दूषणं

यत्पूर्वं विधिना ललाटलिखितं तन्मार्जितुं कः क्षमः ।।

Patraṃ Naiva Yadā Karīlaviṭape Doṣo Vasantasya Kiṃ
Nolūko'pyavalokate Yadi Divā Sūryasya Kiṃ Dūṣaṇam.
Varṣā Naiva Patanti Cātakamukhe Meghasya Kiṃ Dūṣaṇaṃ
Yatpūrvaṃ Vidhinā Lalāṭalikhitaṃ Tanmārjituṃ Kaḥ Kṣamaḥ.

Why does the bamboo sprout lack leaves in the spring? If the owl can't see during the day, what does the sun have to do with it? Is it the fault of the clouds that the chatak bird doesn't receive any rainfall in its mouth? Who has the authority to alter the markings that Lord Brahma made on our foreheads when we were born?

जलबिन्दुनिपातेन क्रमशः पूर्यते घटः ।
स हेतुः सर्वविद्यानां धर्मस्य च धनस्य च ।।

Jalabindunipātena Kramaśaḥ Pūryate Ghaṭaḥ.
Sa Hetuḥ Sarvavidyānāṃ Dharmasya Ca Dhanasya Ca.

As individual droplets will fill a pot gradually so will knowledge, virtue and wealth be gradually obtained.

वयसः परिणामेऽपि यः खलः खल एव सः ।
सम्पक्वमपि माधुर्यं नोपयातीन्द्रवारुणम् ।।

Vayasaḥ Pariṇāme'pi Yaḥ Khalaḥ Khala Eva Saḥ.
Sampakvamapi Mādhuryaṃ Nopayātīndravāruṇam.

Like the Indra-Varuna fruit, which does not turn sweet no matter how ripe it may get, a man who is evil even in old age is actually a fool.

आयुः कर्म च वित्तं च विद्या निधनमेव च ।
पञ्चैतानि हि सृज्यन्ते गर्भस्थस्यैव देहिनः ।।

Āyuḥ Karma Ca Vittaṃ Ca Vidyā Nidhanameva Ca.
Pañcaitāni Hi Sṛjyante Garbhasthasyaiva Dehinaḥ.

These five aspects of the future of the unborn child in his mother's womb are already set in stone: his life expectancy, his activities, his acquisition of money and knowledge, and his death.

अनागतविधाता च प्रत्युत्पन्नमतिस्तथा ।
द्वावेतौ सुखमेधेते यद्भविष्यो विनश्यति ।।

Anāgatavidhātā Ca Pratyutpannamatistathā.
Dvāvetau Sukhamedhete Yadbhaviṣyo Vinaśyati.

He who plans for the future and deftly handles any eventuality is content; yet, the fatalist who relies solely on luck is destroyed.

खनित्वा हि खनित्रेण भूतले वारि विन्दति ।
तथा गुरुगतां विद्यां शुश्रूषुरधिगच्छति ।।

Khanitvā Hi Khanitreṇa Bhūtale Vāri Vindati.
Tathā Gurugatāṃ Vidyāṃ Śuśrūṣuradhigacchati.

Similar to how a guy must use a shovel to dig for water underground, a student must use the service provided in order to learn from his preceptor.

सन्तोषस्त्रिषु कर्तव्यः स्वदारे भोजने धने ।
त्रिषु चौव न कर्तव्योऽध्ययने जपदानयोः ।।

Santoṣastriṣu Kartavyaḥ Svadāre Bhojane Dhane.
Triṣu Caiva Na Kartavyo'dhyayane Japadānayoḥ.

The following three things should satisfy one: one's own wife, food provided by Providence and money earned by sincere labour. However, the following three things should never satisfy one: study, reciting the holy names of the Lord (japa) and charity.

पृथिव्यां त्रीणि रत्नानि जलमन्नं सुभाषितम् ।
मूढैः पाषाणखण्डेषु रत्नसंज्ञा विधीयते ।।

Pṛthivyāṃ Trīṇi Ratnāni Jalamannaṃ Subhāṣitam.
Mūḍhaiḥ Pāṣāṇakhaṇḍeṣu Ratnasaṃjñā Vidhīyate.

The only three priceless jewels on this planet are food, water and melodious words, but foolish people have declared that stones like diamonds are the most valuable.

बहूनां चैव सत्त्वानां समवायो रिपुञ्जयः ।
वर्षाधाराधरो मेघस्तृणैरपि निवार्यते ।।

Bahūnāṃ Caiva Sattvānāṃ Samavāyo Ripuñjayaḥ.
Varṣādhārādharo Meghastṛṇairapi Nivāryate.

Even though they are little in size individually, the community may overwhelm the adversary in vast numbers because the grass roof's collective capacity to prevent heavy rain allows them to do so.

उर्व्यां कोऽपि महीधरो लघुतरो दोर्भ्यां धृतो
लीलया तेन त्वं दिवि भूतले च सततं गोवर्धनो गीयसे ।
त्वां त्रैलोक्यधरं वहामि कुचयोरग्रे न तद्गण्यते
किं वा केशव भाषणेन बहुना पुण्यैर्यशो लभ्यते ।।

Urvyāṃ Ko'pi Mahīdharo Laghutaro Dorbhyāṃ Dhṛto
Līlayā Tena Tvaṃ Divi Bhūtale Ca Satataṃ Govardhano Gīyase.
Tvāṃ Trailokyadharaṃ Vahāmi Kucayoragre Na Tadgaṇyate
Kiṃ Vā Keśava Bhāṣaṇena Bahunā Puṇyairyaśo Labhyate.

Krishna became renowned as Girdhari after lifting the Govardhan mountain with just one finger, and the peak itself gained recognition and became a global object of adoration. However, Braj's Gopis raised Krishna in his youth, though no one is aware of their identity. This demonstrates how fate plays a role in fame.

न निर्मितो न चौव न दृष्टपूर्वो
न श्रूयते हेममयः कुरंगः ।
तथाऽपि तृष्णा रघुनन्दनस्य
विनाशकाले विपरीतबुद्धिः ॥

Na Nirmito Na Caiva Na Dṛṣṭapūrvo
Na Śrūyate Hemamayaḥ Kuraṃgaḥ.
Tathā'pi Tṛṣṇā Raghunandanasya
Vināśakāle Viparītabuddhiḥ.

By chance, someone may get in a prominent position yet not be respected. However, a person with morality is recognized in society even if they are not wealthy. In a similar vein, even if a crow were to occupy the highest skyscraper, it would not be regarded as an eagle.

पुस्तकप्रत्ययाधीतं नाधीतं गुरुसन्निधौ ।
सभामध्ये न शोभन्ते जारगर्भा इव स्त्रियः ॥

Pustakapratyayādhītaṃ Nādhītaṃ Gurusannidhau.
Sabhāmadhye Na Śobhante Jāragarbhā Iva Striyaḥ.

Similar to how an illegitimate kid is not respected in society, a scholar who has learnt through the study of countless books without the blessing of a genuine spiritual teacher does not stand out among a gathering of highly knowledgeable men.

दानेन पाणिर्न तु कङ्कणेन
स्नानेन शुद्धिर्न तु चन्दनेन ।
मानेन तृप्तिर्न तु भोजनेन

ज्ञानेन मुक्तिर्न तु मुण्डनेन ॥

Dānena Pāṇirna Tu Kaṅkaṇena
Snānena Śuddhirna Tu Candanena.
Mānena Tṛptirna Tu Bhojanena
Jñānena Muktirna Tu Muṇḍanena.

One does not become clean by merely smearing sandalwood paste on the body as one does by taking a bath; one does not become satisfied by dinner as one does by having respect shown to him; and salvation is not attained by self-adornment but by cultivating spiritual knowledge. The hand is not ornamented by ornaments as it is by charitable offerings.

आहारनिद्राभयमैथुनानि
समानि चौतानि नृणां पशूनाम् ।
ज्ञानं नराणामधिको विशेषो
ज्ञानेन हीनाः पशुभिः समानाः ॥

Āhāranidrābhayamaithunāni
Samāni Caitāni Nṛṇāṃ Paśūnām.
Jñānaṃ Narāṇāmadhiko Viśeṣo
Jñānena Hīnāḥ Paśubhiḥ Samānāḥ.

Men and animals are similar in that they eat, sleep, fear and mate. Persons are superior to animals in that they possess discretionary knowledge; thus, dishonest men who lack knowledge or opinion should be viewed as animals.

पुस्तकस्था तु या विद्या परहस्तगतं धनं ।
कार्यकाले समुत्पन्ने न सा विद्या न तद्धनम् ॥

Pustakasthā Tu Yā Vidyā Parahastagataṃ Dhanaṃ.
Kāryakāle Samutpanne Na Sā Vidyā Na Taddhanam.

When the need for them comes, someone whose riches is

held by others and whose knowledge is limited to books will be unable to employ either wealth or knowledge.

CHANAKYA SUTRAS

1. सुखस्य मूलं धर्मः ॥
   Righteous conduct is the root of happiness.
   The state and its ruler should have proper knowledge of their dharma (proper duty) to make its functioning bring happiness to the people.
2. धर्मस्य मूलमर्थः ॥
   Practicing dharma requires finance.
   Financial stability ensures proper discharge of the duties in a state.
3. अर्थस्य मूलं राज्यम् ॥
   The state's welfare is rooted in good finance.
4. राज्यमूलमिन्द्रियजयः ॥
   The cornerstone of a state's wellbeing is control over senses and input from the people. The government should modify its policies as necessary in light of the input it gets from the populace.
5. इन्द्रियजयस्य मूलं विनयः ॥
   Humility heps control the senses. When the state authorities deal with people with humility they get proper and right response from the people.
6. विनयस्य मूलं वृद्धोपसेवा ॥
   The essence of humility is in the service of the elderly.

When one renders honest service to elders, one learns the worth of humility.

7. वृद्धसेवाया विज्ञानम् ॥

By serving elders, one gets the true wisdom.

8. विज्ञानेनात्मानं सम्पादयेत् ॥

The ruler (or other authority) can do their tasks more effectively when they have true knowledge.

9. सम्पादितात्मा जितात्मा भवति ॥

The king who can control his senses and knows his duties well can rule efficiently. Hence he gets all prosperity.

10. जितात्मा सर्वार्थैः संयुज्यते ॥

He who can control his senses will get all wishes fulfilled. He gets wealth and prosperity in abundance.

11. स्वामिसम्पत् प्रकृतिसम्पदं करोति ॥

Prosperity of the king (the ruling authority) leads to the prosperity of people.

12. प्रकृतिसम्पदा ह्यनायकमपि राज्यं नीयते ॥

A kingdom without a king works well if its people are prosperous.

13. प्रकृतिकोपः सर्वकोपेभ्यो गरीयान् ॥

The wrath of the people of a kingdom is the worst kind of wrath.

14. अविनीतस्वामिभावादस्वामिभावः श्रेयान् ॥

Instead of a ruler who lacks humility, it is preferable to have none. It is worse to have an uncaring king than none at all.

15. सम्पाद्यात्मानमन्विच्छेत् सहायान् ॥

A king who is able can train his assistant efficiently and then can rule effectively.

16. नाऽसहास्य मन्त्रनिश्चयः ॥

A ruler cannot make wise decisions without competent advisors.

17. नैकं चक्रं परिभ्रमति ॥

The chariot cannot be moved by only one wheel. A king cannot operate effectively alone. He needs the help of his competent cabinet. The two wheels of the state chariot are the king and his cabinet.

18. सहाय: समो दु:खसुखयो: ॥

In both good times and bad, the assistant (or minister to a king) should support the master. In difficult circumstances, the assistant shouldn't forsake the master.

19. मानी प्रतिमानिनमात्मद्वितीयं मन्त्रिणमुत्पादयेत् ॥

A wise ruler must examine all the advantages and disadvantages of a difficult situation before acting and coming to a conclusion.

20. अविनीतं स्नेहमात्रेण न मन्त्रे कुर्वीत ॥

No matter how close you are to a headstrong person, never make him your closest confidant. A person with a strong personality might be pushed to reveal even the most well hidden secrets.

21. श्रुतवन्तमुपधाशुद्धं मन्त्रिणं कुर्वीत ॥

As a minister, a ruler should only pick someone who is well-educated and of good reputation. A minister must have an open mind and unwavering commitment to his king.

22. मन्त्रमूला: सर्वारम्भा: ॥

Before starting any assignment as a ruler, long deliberations should be indispensable.

23. मन्त्रसंवरणे कार्यसिद्धिर्भवति ॥

Success in an assignment is only possible if the previous discussions are kept as tightly guarded secrets.

24. मन्त्रनि:स्राव: सर्वम् नाशयति ॥

The secrets of the state should be conveyed in hushed tones. Any chance of leaking will damage the projects.

25. प्रमादाद् द्विषतां वशमुपयास्यति ॥
Callousness can expose the state's secrets to the enemy. As a result, the state must tightly guard its secrets.

26. सर्वद्वारेभ्यो मन्त्रो रक्षितव्यः ॥
The state's secrets must be protected from any conceivable leaking. Allow no avenue for the transmission of such secrets.

27. मन्त्रसम्पदा हि राज्यं विवर्धते ॥
Protection of the state's secrets ensures its perpetual prosperity.

28. (i) श्रेष्ठतमां मन्त्रगुपितमाहुः ॥
It is best to keep the state's secrets always closely guarded.
(ii) कार्याकार्य प्रदीपो मन्त्रः ॥
In the same way that a lamp illuminates the path in the dark, so does the state administration when their king is confused; his ministers will always participate in prudent discussion in times of obscurity.

29. मन्त्रचक्षुषा परच्छिद्राण्यवलोकयन्ति
The king gets the vision through deliberations with his cabinet to get an insight into his enemy's weaknesses.

30. मन्त्रकाले न मत्सरः कर्तव्यः ॥
While deliberating on state matters, the ruler should never disregard his cabinet's recommendations or be obstinate in his views.

31. त्रयाणामैकवाक्येऽसम्प्रत्ययः॥
When the king's point of view, the advisor's point of view, and the minister's recommendation all agree on a single decision, the discussions are blessed with success in every state endeavour.

32. कार्याकार्य प्रदीपो मन्त्रः ॥
A minister is an able minister only if he clearly knowa

what needs to be done and what not.

33. षट्कर्णो मन्त्रश्छिद्यते ॥

If a secret falls into six ears, it will inevitably leak. The state secret must be kept between the king and the concerned minister. Because if a third person, no matter how close, is aware of it, it is deemed public knowledge.

34. आपत्सु स्नेहयुक्तं मित्रम् ॥

A true friend maintains loving relationships even when things are bad. A friend in need is a true friend.

35. मित्रसंग्रहणे बलं सम्पद्यते ॥

A group of worthy friends make an individual powerful.

36. बलवान् अलब्धलाभे प्रयतेत ॥

A mighty ruler seeks the impossible. Only a powerful ruler can afford to be that bold. He attempts to do something impossible in order to increase his might and glory.

37. अलब्धलाभो नालसस्य ॥

A difficult ambition is out of reach for the lazy. It is impossible for them to obtain any unreachable advantage since they make no effort.

38. अलसेन लब्धमपि रक्षितुं न शक्यते ॥

The lazy can't even protect the advantage already received.

39. न चालसस्ययुक्तस्य रक्षितं विवर्धते ॥

The lazy, owing to their lack of efforts, can't ensure the growth of their assets.

40. न भृत्यान् पोषयति ॥

Lazy kings do not even make their servants work.

41. अलब्धलाभादिचतुष्टयं राजतन्त्रम् ॥

A state must assure four unattainable gains: acquiring what it lacks, ensuring its security once achieved, initiating the growth of that asset, and exchanging that gain for something more valuable to the state.

42. तच्च राज्यतन्त्रमायतं नीतिशास्त्रेषु ॥

The structure to formulate the state policy should always be a part of the state-administration.

43. राज्यतन्त्रेष्वायत्तौ मन्त्रावापौ॥

The structure for developing domestic and international policy must be an integral aspect of state management.

44. मन्त्रं स्वविषये कृत्येष्वायत्तम् ॥

Administration policies must cater to the interior matters of the state.

45. आवापो मण्डले सन्निविष्टः ॥

Foreign policy must cater to dealing with the issues related to foreign countries.

46. सन्धिविग्रहयोर्योनिर्मण्डलम् ॥

Pacts and accords with foreign countries are a constant source of contention. The king must be always mindful of these relations with other countries. Only then will he be able to benefit from them at the appropriate time.

47. नीतिशास्त्रानुगो राजा ॥

The competency of a monarch is measured not only by the formulation of appropriate policies, but also by their ethical implementation. The king must not deviate from the policies he has established. For this may persuade his ministers to follow in his footsteps, breeding indiscipline in the state administration.

48. अनन्तरप्रकृतिः शत्रुः ॥

The countries at the border with which frequent skirmishes happen eventually turn into enemies.

49. एकान्तरितं मित्रमिष्यते ॥

Countries which are similar turn into friends.

50. हेतुतः शत्रुमित्रे भविष्यतः ॥

People become friends or foes for a variety of reasons. Bonding or animosity cannot occur without a reason.

51. हीयमानेन स सन्धिं कुर्वीत ॥

The weak must have a peace-treaty as soon as possible.

52. तेजो हि सन्धानहेतुस्तदर्थिनाम् ॥

A treaty's binding cause is the strength of two peacemakers. A pact is long lasting when two countries have equal strength and influence.

53. नातप्तलोहं लोहेन सन्धत्ते ॥

Two iron pieces must be heated before they may be joined. A long-term treaty can bind two countries of equal power.

54. बलवान् हीनेन विगृह्णीयात् ॥

The mighty always target the weak. Any attack on the more powerful will lead to an adverse outcome.

55. न ज्यायसा समेन वा ॥

Never attack someone who is stronger or more powerful than you. Before engaging in any aggressive behaviour, it is important to gauge one's own power. Any violent engagement should be postponed until one is certain of having an advantage over one's enemy.

56. हस्तिनः पादयुद्धमिव बलवद्विग्रहः ॥

Fighting a stronger opponent is analogous to troops on foot facing an elephant brigade. It just reflects a suicide attempt.

57. आमपात्रमापेन सह विनश्यति ॥

The collision of two pots composed of raw soil results in their disintegration. If two foes of undeveloped strength battle, both will perish.

58. अरिप्रयत्नमभिसमीक्ष्यात्मरक्षया वसेत् ॥

The enemy's efforts should be constantly evaluated. Secret intelligence and other available techniques should be used to keep oneself up to speed on the operations of one's enemy. Never underestimate your opponent's strength.

59. सन्धायैकतो वा यायात् ॥

Even if you have a treaty with the neighbouring country, keep an eye on its operations through constant surveillance.

60. अमित्रविरोधादात्मरक्षामावसेत् ॥

Always monitor the actions of the enemy's spies.

61. शक्तिहीनो बलवन्तमाश्रयेत् ॥

A less powerful king should seek shelter from a more powerful king.

62. दुर्बलाश्रयो दुःखमावहति ॥

Granting shelter to weak brings in suffering and pain.

63. अग्निवद् राजानमाश्रयेत् ॥

Seek the protection of a ruler with utmost caution, as one would seek the safety of fire. If one is not cautious, fire may burn, and the king can punish.

64. राज्ञः प्रतिकूलं नाचरेत् ॥

Your behaviour should not run against the king's orders.

65. नोद्धतवेशधरः स्यात् ॥

It is never acceptable to dress inappropriately. Regardless of one's perspective, the outfit should not be an eyesore to the audience.

66. न देवचरितं चरेत् ॥

One must not imitate God's demeanour or lifestyle. You can't emulate God no matter how much money or alternative you have.

67. द्वयोरपीर्ष्यतोर्द्वैधीभावकुर्वीत ॥

Always sow a seed of tension between the people nursing jealousy for you.

68. न व्यसनपरस्य कार्यावाप्तिः ॥

A person who is hooked to a substance or has harmful habits will never be able to improve. Their addiction will prevent them from giving their whole concentration to any task they embark on.

69. इन्द्रियवशवर्तिनो नास्ति कार्यावाप्तिः ॥

Even though a ruler controls a worthy army, he will fall if his senses govern him. Whatever sensuous weakness will negate any advantage his powerful army may earn.

70. नास्ति कार्यं द्युतप्रवृत्तस्य ॥

Any person addicted to gambling will never be able to complete any projects in time.

71. मृगयापरस्य धर्मार्थौ विनश्यतः ॥

Hunting addicts inevitably lose their religious beliefs and money. Addiction is such a driving passion that people would go against their religious beliefs in order to win their stake.

72. अर्थेषु पानव्यसनी न गण्यते ॥

Longing for amassing wealth is not wrong since all want to be rich.

73. न कामासक्तस्य कार्यानुष्ठानम् ॥

A lecherous person can not accomplish anything.

74. अग्निदहादपि विशिष्टं वाक्पारुष्यम् ॥

Rigid language burns more than a fire. For a wound caused by fire may be healed, but a hurt created by a harsh comment cannot.

75. दण्डपारुष्यात् सर्वजनद्वेष्यो भवति ॥

When an innocent person is severely punished, he or she becomes resentful and an adversary of the punishing authority.

76. अर्थतोषिणं श्रीः परित्यजति ॥

A king who is satiated with his wealth will have goddess Laxmi and his riches soon desert him.

77. अमित्रो दण्डनीत्यामायत्तः ॥

The structure of punishment determines the enemy's survivability. The harsher the punishment, the less the chances of enemies.

78. दण्डनीतिमनुष्ठन् प्रजाः संरक्षति ॥

A state protects the public by judiciously enforcing the policy and punishment.

79. दण्डः सर्वसम्पदा योजयति ॥

Proper punishment and policy implementation enables improved administration and the smooth operation of law and order. As a result, the state's industry and trade benefit.

80. दण्डाभावे त्रिवर्गाभावः ॥

The lack of an appropriate punishment policy degrades the sensibility of even state ministers. When those in positions of authority in a state have no fear of the criminal law, they begin engaging in reckless corrupt acts that undermine the state.

81. दण्डभयादकार्याणि न कुर्वन्ति ॥

The absence of a functional penal code encourages illegal actions within the state. When people are not afraid of punishment, they engage in illegal behaviours without thinking about the consequences.

82. दण्डनीत्यामायत्तमात्मरक्षणम् ॥

The security of the people is mostly determined by the state's punishment policy. The stricter the rules, the less need there will be for self-defense.

83. आत्मनि रक्षिते सर्वं रक्षितं भवति ॥

Proper self-defense protects the safety of everyone. It is considered that if the ruler is adequately guarded, the subjects will be well guarded as well.

84. आत्मायत्तौ वृद्धिविनाशौ ॥

The choice between growth and disaster is always one's own. Nobody can assure someone's progress if they are self-sabotaging; and nobody can stop someone who is determined to grow.

85. दण्डनीत्यादि विज्ञाने प्रणीयते ॥

Any punishment must be administered with caution. The state cannot simply implement the criminal code without taking into account a person's basic nature and past behaviour.

86. दुर्बलोऽपि राजा नावमन्तव्यः ॥

Even if the king is feeble, he should never be dishonoured. A king is a state institution. Even if the ruler is weak, he deserves respect since he represents the state. Dishonouring him is tantamount to disgracing oneself and one's nation.

87. नास्त्यग्नेर्दौर्बल्यम् ॥

Fire is never weak. Even a tiny cinder can burn a huge jungle to ashes.

88. दण्डेन प्रणीयते वृत्तिः ॥

The king generates his income from the ethics of the administration of the state.

89. वृत्तिमूलोऽर्थलाभः ॥

Gain is the primary goal of every endeavour. All job is done in order to make a profit and earn money.

90. अर्थमूलौ धर्मकामौ ॥

The root of dharma (religious belief) and Kama (satiation of desires) is Artha (wealth).

91. अर्थमूलम् कार्यम् ॥

Money is the foundation of all the projects.

92. यत्नप्रयत्नात् कार्यसिद्धिर्भवति स उपायः ॥

With financial capacity, one can achieve objectives even with minimal efforts.

93. उपायपूर्वं कार्यं न दुष्करं स्यात् ॥

To tackle any difficulty, one must have genuine devotion and drive. Any problem may be solved with proper preparation.

94. अनुपायपूर्वं कार्यं कृतमपि विनश्यति ॥

If one attempts to solve a problem without commitment and dedication, what is accomplished is also lost.

95. कार्यार्थिनामुपाय एव सहायः ॥

Proper planning is extremely helpful for industrialists.

96. कार्यं पुरुषकारेण लक्ष्यं सम्पद्यते ॥

If a job becomes one's sole aim, it gets completed due to the determination.

97. पुरुषकारमनुवर्तते दैवम् ॥

Fortune favours those who are brave.

98. दैवं विना अतिप्रयत्नं करोति यत्तद् विफलम् ॥

God helps those who help themselves.

99. अनीहमानस्य वृत्तिर्न सम्पद्यते ॥

Fatalists are doomed in life. Those who wait for their fortunes to turn in their favour never get to earn a living.

100. पूर्वं निश्चित्य पश्चात्कार्यमारभेत ॥

Consider every advantage and disadvantage before starting any job, and then choose your line of action.

101. कार्यान्तरे दीर्घसूत्रता न कर्तव्या ॥

Do not let up until the entire task is finished. The completion of tasks will be delayed if you take breaks mid-task.

102. न चलचित्तस्य कार्यावाप्तिः ॥

A fickle mind can never concentrate and complete a job successfully.

103. हस्तगतावमाननात् कार्यव्यतिक्रमो भवति ॥

Not using the needed resources properly interferes with the completion of the work.

104. दोषवर्जितानि कार्याणि दुर्लभानि ॥
Completing a task flawlessly is a rare happening.

105. दुरनिबन्धं कार्यं न आरभेत ॥
One must not take up the job whose end is not assured before hand.

106. कालवित् कार्यं साधयेत् ॥
Whoever chooses the best moment to complete a work always moves in the direction of success. Every job has a best time to be completed.

107. कालातिक्रमात् काल एव फलं पिबति ॥
Time finally annuls the outcomes of a project when there is interference with its progression. Any task that is completed carelessly will be of poor quality.

108. क्षणं प्रति कालविक्षेपं न कुर्यात् सर्वकृतेषु ॥
When performing duties, not even a single second should be lost. It is impossible to make up for lost time at the beginning with time added afterwards.

109. देशकालविभागौ ज्ञात्वा कार्यमारभेत ॥
Finding the location and timing of a task is necessary before doing it. Each piece of art has a certain meaning depending on the setting and moment it is created. It could be acceptable in one place or at one moment, but it might be dangerous in another place or at a different time.

110. दैवहीनं कार्यं सुसाधमपि दुस्साधं भवति ॥
An easy work becomes difficult for an unfortunate person.

111. नीतिज्ञो देशकालौ परीक्षेत ॥
The diplomats must examine the contemporary situation of a country before making any decision.

112. परीक्ष्यकारिणि श्रीश्चिरं तिष्ठति ॥
When a project is started after its potential effects have

been tested, the benefits are typically felt for a very long period. A campaign has advantages for the person who evaluates the prospective outcome beforehand after determining its effectiveness in terms of time and location.

113. सर्वाश्च सम्पदः सर्वोपायेन परिगृह्णीयात् ॥

All resources must be gathered and preserved in any way that is practical. A ruler who is responsible for the prosperity of his realm must acquire various resources using all available tools since he never knows which will be useful later on.

114. भाग्यवन्तमप्यपरीक्ष्यकारिणं श्रीः परित्यजति ॥

Even a lucky individual who works without anticipating the results of that labour would lose favour with the goddess of wealth and resources, Lakshmi.

115. ज्ञात्वाऽनुमानैश्च परीक्षा कर्तव्या ॥

When analysing the potential outcomes of a task that needs to be completed, knowledge and guesswork must both be employed.

116. यो यस्मिन्कर्मणि कुशलस्तं तस्मिन्नेव योजयेत् ॥

A particular job must be assigned to a plausible performer on the basis of his expertise.

117. दुस्साधमपि सुसाधं करोत्युपायज्ञः ॥

He who knows the tricks of the trade makes even the most difficult tasks easy.

118. अज्ञानिना कृतमपि न बहुमन्तव्यं यादृच्छिकत्वात् ॥

Any job accomplished by an ignorant fellow must not be given any importance.

119. कृमयोऽपो हि कदाचित् रूपान्तराणि कुर्वन्ति ॥

Even woodworms may create a variety of designs by accidently piercing the wood, but they cannot in any way be considered artists. It's only a coincidence, just as an uninformed idiot may come up with something interesting, but it shouldn't be given any weight.

120. सिद्धस्यैव कार्यस्य प्रकाशनं कर्तव्यम् ॥

Only completed and successful work should be made public. Publicizing an incomplete task might persuade the opponent to obstruct it in the middle.

121. ज्ञानवतामपि दैवमानुषदोषात् कार्याणि दुष्यन्ति ॥

Even the achievements of the knowledgeable people can get sullied by the interference of fate or men.

122. दैवं दोषं शान्तिकर्मणा प्रतिषेधयेत् ॥

Natural catastrophes must be handled calmly (and not panic). The terrible acts of Providence, such as earthquakes, floods, droughts, tsunamis, etc., inevitably foster a sense of hopelessness in the minds of prospective victims, which makes the situation much worse.

123. मानुषीं कार्यविपत्तिं कौशलेन विनिवारयेत् ॥

The difficulties in work borne by men should be solved with wisdom.

124. कार्यविपत्तौ दोषान् वर्णयन्ति बालिशाः ॥

They are foolish if they begin blaming others for their problems at work. They should strive to identify the root of the problem, but when fools start pointing the finger at one another, the problem may worsen.

125. कार्यार्थिना दाक्षिण्यं न कर्तव्यम् ॥

Don't be kind towards the people who can harm you.

126. क्षीरार्थि वत्सो मातुरूधः प्रतिहन्ति ॥

Even a calf will assault its mother cow's udder when it seeks milk. The needs of the body subdue the affection.

127. अप्रयत्नात् कार्यविपत्तिर्भवेत् ॥

Lack of sincerity in efforts ruins the work being carried out.

128. न दैवमात्रप्रमाणानां कार्यसिद्धिः ॥

The one who relies on luck never achieves success in his/her assignments.

129. कार्यबाह्यो न पोषयत्याश्रितान् ॥

Those who shirk their duties are never able to properly care for the individuals who depend on them.

130. यः कार्यं न पश्यति सोऽन्धः ॥

He who cannot perceive his own work is like a blind man. Before beginning a work, one must thoroughly evaluate all the factors.

131. प्रत्यक्षपरोक्षनुमानैः कार्याणि परीक्षेत ॥

With the use of direct or indirect techniques that are accessible, one must assess the job and the methods for carrying it out while prudently supplementing it with fully informed estimates.

132. अपरीक्षकारिणं श्रीः परित्यजति ॥

Because success and any further profits are always denied to those who work without making such rigorous estimates.

133. परीक्ष्य तार्या विपत्तिः ॥

When a problem arises at work, all relevant factors should be carefully reviewed in order to identify and fix the problem.

134. स्वशक्तिं ज्ञात्वा कार्यमारभेत ॥

Initiate any work after assessing your capability of doing it entirely.

135. स्वजनं तर्पयित्वा यश्शेषभोजी सोऽमृतभोजी ॥

The individual who feeds family members and friends before eating anything himself actually participates in making ambrosia from leftovers.

136. सम्यगनुष्ठानादायमुखानि वर्धन्ते ॥

One must not leave any opportunity of enhancing one's resources. This will ensure constant growth.

137. नास्ति भीरोः कार्यचिन्ता ॥
The cowards don't worry about their work or duties. A coward is actually a work-shirker.

138. स्वामिनः शीलं ज्ञात्वा कार्यार्थी कार्यं साधयेत् ॥
Before dedicating themselves to work, those who are working for a master must understand the nature of the master. The smart workers choose how they should work after first evaluating their master's character, including his personality, expectations, and working style.

139. धेनोश्शीलज्ञो हि क्षीरं भुङ्क्ते ॥
Similarly, one who knows the nature of a cow enjoys her milk in the best manner.

140. क्षुद्रे गुह्यप्रकाशनमात्मवान् न कुर्यात् ॥
Never share secrets with someone lacking depth of character.

141. आश्रितैरप्यवमन्यते मृदुस्वभावः ॥
Even his dependents will offend a guy with a compassionate heart. Being kind-hearted might persuade even one's dependents or subordinates to oppose or offend one, which is not good for the state administration.

142. तीक्ष्णदण्डः सर्वेषामुद्वेजनीयो भवति ॥
All of the subjects despise a ruler who punishes his offenders harshly. If a ruler in the state is a sadist, his followers are unlikely to show him any favour. Instead, he will be the object of their animosity.

143. यथार्हदण्डकारी स्यात् ॥
Therefore, the king must punish the offender fairly. Extremely severe punishment may make the ruler the target of his citizens' rage, while excessive indulgence may encourage the offender to act quite audaciously. Therefore, the penalty must be fair and fitting.

144. अल्पसारं श्रुतवन्तमपि न बहुमन्यते लोकः ॥

A frivolous scholar doesn't command any respect in the society.

145. अतिभारः पुरुषमवसादयति ॥

An increased workload may cause the king to become unhappy and anxious. He should give his assistants as much work as their skill set will allow.

146. यः संसदि परदोषं शंसति स स्वदोषबहुत्वमेव प्रख्यापयति ॥

Anyone who criticizes others' inefficiencies in the people's court or in the legislature brings attention to his own shortcomings. Instead than focusing on the individual's insufficiency in court, the issue should be the defects in the government's system.

147. आत्मानमेव नाशयत्यनात्मवतां कोपः ॥

Those who are oblivious of their own skills eventually fail because of their wrath. Fools' wrath eventually hurts their own interests.

148. नास्त्यप्राप्यं सत्यवताम् ॥

For individuals blessed with the virtue of truth, nothing is impossible. The greatest riches, the truth, enables one to reach all of life's peaks.

149. न केवलेन साहसेन कार्यसिद्धिर्भवति ॥

For someone to succeed in life, courage is inadequate. To achieve a goal, one needs skills and resources.

150. व्यसनार्तो विस्मरत्यवश्यकर्तव्यान् ॥

Anyone who indulges in vices falls short of their goals. You shouldn't entrust these folks with any important tasks.

151. नास्त्यनन्तरायः कालविक्षेपे ॥

One's job must be completed at due time because any delay might hamper its completion permanently.

152. असंशयविनाशात् संशयविनाशः श्रेया ॥

It is preferable to experience present devastation than

to anticipate it in the future. To die in what you know will be definite devastation is preferable to dying in a protracted state of confusion.

153. केवलं धनानि निक्षेप्तुं न स्वार्थं ॥

It is selfish to treat someone else's money differently. If you are in possession of someone else's property, treat it with the same level of security as your own. Don't make distinctions between your fortune and that of others since doing so breeds selfishness.

154. दानं धर्मः ॥

Charity is religion. Charity is the essence of religious faith.

155. नार्या आगतोऽर्थः तद्विपरीतमनर्थभावं भजते ॥

Uncivilized people gaining wealth spell doom for the society.

156. यो धर्मार्थौ न व्यर्थयति स कामः ॥

The things that don't strengthen one's religious belief are only attempts to gratify one's carnal needs.

157. तद्विपरीतोऽनर्थसेवी ॥

Money obtained illegally does not, in and of itself, equate to riches. As the money is solely spent in the wrong places, it offers no financial stability.

158. ऋजुस्वभावप्रो जनो दुर्लभः ॥

A simple-minded man is rare. A naïve individual cannot live in society since most people have terrible dispositions.

159. अवमानेनागतमैश्वर्यमवमन्यत एव साधुः ॥

He who does not accept the wealth acquired by illegal means given to him is a real saint.

160. बहूनपि हि गुणानेकदोषो ग्रसति ॥

Even if one has a single flaw, it might nullify all his other good qualities.

161. महात्मना परं साहसं न कर्तव्यम् ।।

A lofty man never relies on other's courage.

162. कदाचिदपि चारित्रं न लङ्घयेत् ।।

One must not violate one's basic foundational characteristics.

163. क्षुधाऽऽर्तो न तृणं चरति सिंहः ।।

A hungry lion would never eat grass.

(This sutra is in relation to the previous one.)

164. प्राणादपि प्रत्ययो रक्षितव्यः ।।

One must protect one's faith even if comes at the cost of one's life.

165. पिशुनो नेता पुत्रदारैरपि त्यज्यते ।।

Backbiting eventually leads to one's own wife and son abandoning him. Even his closest friends can't tolerate it for very long.

166. बालादपि युक्तमर्थं शृणुयात् ।।

Even children should partake as listeners in meaningful conversations.

167. सत्यमप्यश्रद्धेयं न वदेत् ।।

If an unpleasant truth can potentially disturb one's faith, it should not be said.

168. नाल्पदोषाद्बहुगुणास्त्यज्यन्ते ।।

If a virtuous person has a few bad qualities, do not discard him owing to those flaws.

169. विपश्चित्स्वपि सुलभा दोषाः ।।

Even the learned people can make mistakes and be flawed.

170. नास्ति रत्नमखण्डितम् ।।

Even the most precious gem can be flawed.

171. मर्यादातीतं न कदाचिदपि विश्वसेत् ।।

Never rely on a person who does not care for the bounds of virtue.

172. अप्रिये कृते प्रियमपि द्वेष्यं भवति ॥

Even a favour done by an enemy can be harmful. It can prove to be your undoing later on.

173. नमन्त्यपि हि तुलाकोटिः कूपोदकक्षयं करोति ॥

Only the bowed down side of a see-saw can draw water from a well.

174. सतां मतं नातिक्रामेत् ॥

Never go against the advice of honourable people. Their sayings accurately reflect the life-long experience. Therefore, it must never be disregarded.

175. गुणवदाश्रयान् निर्गुणोऽपि गुणी भवति ॥

Even those who lack virtue become virtous in the company of virtues. Therefore, having good company has a noticeable effect.

176. क्षीराश्रितं जलं क्षीरमिव भवति ॥

Immersing of water in milk makes even water as good as milk.

(The thought of the previous Sutra is exemplified here.)

177. मृत्पिण्डेऽपि पाटलिपुष्पं स्वगन्धमुत्पादयति ॥

Even raw earth (or soil) produces fragrance when it comes in touch with flowers.

178. रजतं कनकसङ्गात् कनकं भवति ॥

Silver becomes gold when mixed with gold.

179. उपकर्तर्यपकर्तुमिच्छत्यबुधः ॥

A fool acts foully even with those who do him/her good.

180. न पाप कर्मणामाक्रोशभयम् ॥

A sinful person is not afraid of ill-fame.

181. उत्साहवतां शत्रवोऽपि वशीभवन्ति ॥

Courageous people can even overpower their enemies.

182. विक्रमधना हि राजानः ॥

A king becomes rich with his valourous attitude.

183. नास्त्यालस्यैहिकमामुष्मिकं वा ॥
There is no present or future for someone who is lazy.
184. निरुत्साहाद्दैवं पतति ॥
Absence of enthusiasm can ruin even the fortune bestowed by God.
185. मत्स्यार्थीव जालमुपयुज्यार्थं गृह्णीयात् ॥
Dive into the water and take advantage of it like a fisherman. In a same vein, face challenges head-on to seize the chance they present.
186. अविश्वस्तेषु विश्वसो न कर्तव्यः ॥
Never rely on someone who is a known betrayer.
187. विषं विषमेव सार्वकालम् ॥
Regardless of the circumstance, poison remains poison.
188. अर्थसमादाने वैरिणां सङ्ग एव न कर्तव्यः ॥
To protect one's money, leaving the enemies' company is an essential prerequisite.
189. अर्थसिद्धौ वैरिणं न विश्वसेत् ॥
Never trust your enemies while endeavouring to achieve your target.
190. अर्थाधीन एव नियतसम्बन्धः ॥
Every relationship is characterized with some mutual advantage to be gained.
191. शत्रोरपि सुतः सखा रक्षितव्यः ॥
If you can become friends with the enemy's son, protect him. Treat the son as an ally as you both share the same goals, namely, removing the ruler from the throne.
192. यावच्छत्रोश्छिद्रं पश्यति तावद्धस्तेन वा स्कन्धेन वा संवाह्यः ॥
Deceive your enemy through artificial behaviour till you find his weaknesses.
193. शत्रुंछिद्रं प्रहरेत् ॥
Attack on your enemy by locating and targetting his weakness.

194. आत्मछिद्रं न प्रकाशयेत् ।।

Never disclose your weakness in front of anyone.

195. छिद्रप्रहारिणः शत्रवोऽपि ।।

Enemies will always target your weaknesses. Hence, don't let them be revealed at all.

196. हस्तगतमपि शत्रुं न विश्वसेत् ।।

Never rely on enemy even when you have captured him/her.

197. स्वजनस्य दुर्वृतं निवारयेत् ।।

Try to get rid of the flaws in your close one's character.

198. स्वजनावमानोऽपि मनस्विनां दुःखमावहति ।।

Thoughful people feel sad when their close ones are insulted.

199. एकाङ्गदोषः पुरुषमवसादयति ।।

One feels agony even if a single part of one's body is flawed.

200. शत्रुं जयति सुवृत्तता ।।

Only noble habits can win one's enemies.

201. निकृतिप्रिया नीचाः ।।

A mean fellow is of trouble for a noble man.

202. नीचस्य मतिर्न दातव्या ।।

No advice should be given to vile people for they'll never pay any heed to it.

203. नीचेषु विश्वासो न कर्तव्यः ।।

One should never rely upon a mischief monger.

204. सुपूजितोऽपि दुर्जनः पीडयत्येव ।।

Even though honoured, a mischief-monger will only give trouble.

205. चन्दनदीनपि दावोऽग्निर्दहत्येव ।।

The forest fire burns even the priced wood like sandalwood.

206. कदाऽपि कमपि पुरुषं नावमन्येत ।।

A noble man should never be insulted.

207. क्षन्तव्यमिति पुरुषं न बाधेत ॥

Never make a person who is to be pardoned sad.

208. भर्त्राऽधिकं रहस्युक्तं वक्तुमिच्छन्त्यबुधः ॥

Only fools can reveal the secrets told to them in private by their masters.

209. अनुरागस्तु फलेन (हितेन) सूच्यते ॥

Affection is revealed not with words but through actions.

210. आज्ञाफलमैश्वर्यम् ॥

Opulence's result is revealed by the compliance of its order.

211. दातव्यमपि बालिशः परिक्लेशेन दास्यति ॥

Fools will give trouble to their benefactors as well.

212. महदैश्वर्यं प्राप्यापि अधृतिमान् विनश्यति ॥

Impatient people perish even with great wealth and opulence.

213. नास्त्यधृतेरैहिकमामुष्मिकं वा ॥

Impatient people have no present or future.

214. न दुर्जनैः सह संसर्गः कर्तव्यः ॥

Always avoid company of the mischief makers.

215. शौण्डहस्तगतं पयोऽप्यवमन्यते जनः ॥

If supplied by a drunken person, even milk is unacceptable. Always be on the lookout for non-virtuous people doing seemingly good gestures.

216. कार्यसङ्कटेष्वर्थव्यवसायिनी बुद्धिः ॥

Intelligent people can detect their benefit even amidst crisis.

217. मितभोजनं स्वास्थ्यम् ॥

A sensible diet is the key to good health.

218. पथ्यमप्यपथ्याजीर्णे नाश्नीयात् ॥

If heavy food causes constipation, avoid eating easily digestible food as well.

219. जीर्णभोजिनं व्याधिर्नोपसर्पति ॥

If the food is properly digested, one will not get ill.

220. जीर्णशरीरे वर्धमानं व्याधिं नोपेक्षेत ॥

Never neglect even a minor ailment when the body is weak, emaciated and old.

221. अजीर्णे भोजनं दुःखम् ॥

Eating any food which causes indigestion can lead to trouble.

222. शत्रोरपि विशिष्यते व्याधिः ॥

Getting a disease is far more dangerous than an enemy.

223. दानं निधानमनुगामि ॥

Charity should be made according to once's capacity.

224. पटुतरेऽपि तृष्णापरे सुलभमतिसन्धानम् ॥

It is only the cunning and greedy people who try to get intimate for selfish motives.

225. तृष्णया मतिश्छाद्यते ॥

Greed affects one's intelligence.

226. कार्यबहुत्वे बहुफलमायतिकं कुर्यात् ॥

If one has a variety of work options, one should pursue the one that offers the greatest potential for reward first.

227. स्वयमेवावस्कन्नं कार्यं निरीक्षेत ॥

Reexamine the work that you or others did. Never fully rely on someone for a job, and always double-check your work.

228. मूर्खेषु साहसं नियतम् ॥

Fools are by nature courageous.

229. मूर्खेषु विवादो न कर्तव्यः ॥

Never lock horns with fools.

230. मूर्खेषु मूर्खवदेव कथयेत् ॥

Talk to fools in their own language.

231. आयसैरायसं छेद्यम् ॥

Iron can get cut by iron only.

232. नास्त्यधीमतस्सखा ॥
Fools have no friends.
233. धर्मेण धार्यते लोकः ॥
One must follow dharma in this world.
234. प्रेतमपि धर्माधर्मावनुगच्छतः ॥
Even ghosts and spirits follow their dharma.
235. दया धर्मस्य जन्मभूमिः ॥
The foundation of dharma is compassion for others.
236. धर्ममूले सत्यदाने ॥
An honest donation is the root of dharma.
237. धर्मेण जयति लोकान् ॥
He who follows dharma truthfully will gain victory in all the worldly endeavours.
238. मृत्यरपि धर्मिष्ठं रक्षति ॥
Even death can't destruct a person who has stuck to his faith firmly.
239. धर्माद्विपरीतं पापं यत्र यत्र प्रसज्यते तत्र धर्मावमतिरेव महती प्रसज्यते ॥
Those who don't rely on their faith spread sin and cause great dishonour to dharma.
240. उपस्थितविनाशानां प्रकृतिः आकारेण कार्येण च लक्ष्यते ॥
Impending doom is always conveyed by nature's indications.
241. आत्मविनाशं सूचयत्यधर्मबुद्धिः ॥
When a person behaves contrary to their religious beliefs, it foreshadows oncoming self-destructive behaviour.
242. पिशुनवादिनो रहस्यं कुतः ॥
Never disclose your secrets to a back-biter.
243. पररहस्यं नैव श्रोतव्यम् ॥
Never try to know another's secret.
244. वल्लभस्य स्वार्थपरत्वमधर्मयुक्तम् ॥
The master must avoid becoming overly cordial with the subordinates since they can act contemptuously

and go beyond what is proper.

245. स्वजनेष्वप्यतिक्रमो न कर्तव्यः ॥

One should not insult or show contempt to one's near and dear ones.

246. मताऽपि दुष्टा त्याज्या ॥

A mother who is wicked can be deserted.

247. स्वहस्तोऽपि विषदिग्धश्छेद्यः ॥

If your hand has been poisoned, cut it off. Get rid of the bad people from society in the same way, regardless of how dear or near they may be to you.

248. परोऽपि च हितो बन्धुः ॥

If an unknown person is your well-wisher, treat him or her like your kin.

249. कक्षादप्यौषधं गृह्यते ॥

Herbal medication can be found even in a deserted jungle. Get it without hesitation if you can locate something that heals, even if it comes from the most unlikely place.

250. नास्ति चोरेषु विश्वासः ॥

Never rely on thieves.

251. अप्रतीकारेष्वनादरो न कर्तव्यः ॥

Never ignore your enemy even when he might appear indifferent.

252. व्यसनं मनागपि बाधते ॥

Even a minor addiction can be troublesom some time.

253. अमरवदर्थजातमार्जयेत् ॥

Amass wealth while believing oneself to be eternal. One must make every effort to gain riches. Don't give up because you fear you won't live long enough to reap the rewards.

254. अर्थवान् सर्वलोकस्य बहुमतः ॥
The whole world respects a wealthy or a resourceful person.

255. महेन्द्रमप्यर्थहीनं न बहुमन्यते लोकः ॥
The world doesn't respect a king with no wealth or resources.

256. दारिद्र्यं खलु पुरुषस्य सजीवितं मरणम् ॥
Suffering poverty is like being dead even when you are alive.

257. विरूपोऽप्यर्थवान् सुरूपः ॥
Money can transform even an ugly person into looking appealing.

258. अदातारमप्यर्थवन्तमर्थिनो न त्यजन्ति ॥
The beggars don't spare even a miserly man.

259. अकुलीनोऽपि धनवान् कुलीनाद्विशिष्टः ॥
A scion of an aristocratic family with little financial security is preferable than a wealthy member of a lower family.

260. नास्त्यवमानभयमनार्यस्य ॥
A mean person is not afraid of insult.

261. नोद्योगवतां वृत्तिभयम् ॥
Skilled people are not scared of losing their livelihood.

262. न जितेन्द्रियाणां विषयभयम् ॥
Those who keep control over their senses are not afraid of their indulgence in sensual pleasure.

263. न कृतार्थानां मरणभयम् ॥
The righteous do not fear death.

264. कस्यचिदर्थं स्वमिव मन्यते साधुः ॥
A gentleman deems everyone else's wealth as his own. He preserves it as if it belongs to him.

265. परविभवेष्वादरो न कर्तव्यः ॥
One should never greedily seek other's opulence.

266. परविभवेष्वादरोऽपि नाशमूलम् ॥
Seeking the riches of others is the underlying cause of one's downfall. He who covets other people's money brings ruin upon himself since all of his actions will be focused on other people's wealth and he may not be able to accomplish anything on his own.

267. पलालमपि परद्रव्यं न हर्तव्यम् ॥
One shouldn't steal even the smallest belonging of others.

268. परद्रव्यापहरणमात्मद्रव्यनाशहेतुः ॥
Usurping other's wealth leads to destruction of one's own money.

269. न चौर्यात् परं मृत्युपाशः ॥
It is better to die than to steal from someone.

270. यवागूरपि प्राणधारणं करोति काले ॥
Even a dinner of parched grain will be enough to keep you alive. As a result, one should not feel the urge to want other people's money.

271. न मृतस्यौषधं प्रयोजनम् ॥
A dead person requires no medicine.

272. समकाले प्रभुत्वस्यप्रयोजनं भवति ॥
Ensuring one's peace-time becomes the essence of success.

273. नीचस्य विद्याः पापकर्मण्येव तं योजयन्ति ॥
The mean minded always use their education for carrying out sinful activities.

274. पयःपानमपि विषवर्धनं भुजङ्गस्य न त्वमृतं स्यात् ॥
Even feeding a snake milk will only increase the production of venom; it will not produce nectar.

275. न धान्यसमो ह्यर्थः ॥
There is no riches comparable to grain. Because food is the most important essential for living, having access

to grain is the ultimate prosperity.

276. न क्षुधासमः शत्रुः ॥

There is no enemy deadlier than hunger.

277. अकृतेर्नियता क्षुत् ॥

To die of hunger is written in the destiny of lazy people.

278. नास्त्यभक्ष्यं क्षुधितस्य ॥

Nothing is uneatable for a man who is hungry.

279. इन्द्रियाणि प्रतिपदं नरान जरावशान् कुर्वन्ति ॥

Over indulgence in sensory pleasures hastens the onset of the old age.

280. सानुक्रोशं भर्तारमाजीवेत् ॥

Only he who can be considerate to his servants' weals and woes deserves their service.

281. लुब्धसेवी पावकेच्छया खद्योतं धमति ॥

A thoughtless master's servant helps the master by attempting to start a fire in the wood by throwing tough glow worms on it. Similar to this endeavour, serving a callous master is a fruitless endeavour.

282. विशेषज्ञं स्वामिनमाश्रयेत् ॥

One must always seek support from a considerate and skilled master.

283. पुरुषस्य मैथुनं जरा ॥

A man ages faster if he copulates more.

284. स्त्रीणाममैथुनं जरा ॥

A woman ages faster if she doesn't copulate.

285. न नीचोत्तमयोर्विवाहः ॥

Only those with compatible natures and position should form a marriage connection. A person with high aspirations shouldn't wed someone with low morals.

286. अगमयागमनादायुर्यशः पुण्यानि क्षीयन्ते ॥

Copulation with a lady who is not intended for this reason causes a guy to quickly lose his youth, glory, and advantages.

287. नास्त्यहङ्कारसमः शत्रुः ॥

Pride is one's greatest enemy.

288. संसदि शत्रु न परिक्रोशेत ॥

Never express anger at your adversary while attending an assembly. Emotional outbursts in public are rude because they divert the attention of the audience.

289. शत्रुव्यसनं श्रवणसुखम् ॥

Hearing condescending things about one's enemy provides a lot of comfort.

290. अधनस्य बुद्धिर्न विद्यते ॥

A pauper always lacks wisdom.

291. हितमप्यधनस्य वाक्यं न गृह्यते ॥

Nobody pays attention to wise counsel offered by a beggar. Even if someone is extremely intelligent, a pauper does not deserve respect.

292. अधनः स्वभार्ययाऽप्यवमन्यते ॥

A person who isn't able to provide for his family gets insulted by his own wife.

293. पुष्पहीनं सहकारमपि नोपासते भ्रमराः ॥

Even bees desert a flowerless mango tree.

294. विद्या धनमधनानाम् ॥

The wealth of paupers lies in their knowledge.

295. विद्या चोरैरपि न ग्राह्या ॥

Thieves can't steal anyone's knowledge.

296. विद्या सुलभा ख्यातिः ॥

Knowledge spreads one's fame.

297. यशः शरीरं न विनश्यति ॥

One's fame will never get destroyed.

298. यः पराथमन्यमुपसर्पति स सत्पुरुषः ॥

The one who comes ahead for other's benefit is the real man.

299. इन्द्रियाणां प्रशमं शास्त्रम् ॥
Real wisdom may be attained with the use of information that teaches how to manage one's senses and maintain calm.

300. अकार्यप्रवृत्ते: शास्त्राङ्कुशं निवारयति ॥
When evil spreads, the knowledge which teaches to control senses shows its dominance.

301. नीचस्य विद्या नोपेतव्या ॥
The skills of the mean should never be imitated.

302. म्लेच्छभाषणं न शिक्षेत ॥
The language of barbarians should never be learnt. Their vocabulacy is of vile phrases.

303. म्लेच्छानामपि सुवृत्तं ग्राह्यम् ॥
The good qualities, even if they come from the barbarians, should be adopted in one's daily life.

304. गुणे न मत्सर: कर्तव्य: ॥
Never be too lazy in learning good qualities.

305. शत्रोरपि सुगुणो ग्राह्य: ॥
The good qualities of an enemy should be adopted.

306. विषादप्यमृतं ग्राह्यम् ॥
Even if poison has traces of nectar, it should be extracted from it.

307. अवस्थया पुरुष: संमान्यते ॥
Due to one's status, one gets revered. By effectively carrying out one's responsibilities, one rises in the social hierarchy.

308. स्थान एव नरा: पूज्यन्ते ॥
A man is worshipped due to the qualities he possesses.

309. आर्यवृतमनुतिष्ठेत् ॥
One should always try to maintain the best behaviour.

310. कदापि मर्यादां नातिक्रामेत् ॥
Never violate your limits.

311. नास्त्यर्घः ओउरुषरत्नस्य ॥
Man is a gem that cannot be measured. He is a collection of innumerable traits, the value of which cannot be expressed in material terms.

312. न स्त्रीरत्नसमं रत्नम् ॥
There is nothing as precious as a woman. She is an incomparable gem.

313. सुदुर्लभं हि रत्नम् ॥
It is rare to find a precious gem. A worthy man and a worthy woman are rare gems.

314. अयशो भयं भयेषु ॥
Ill-fame should be the deadliest fear for a man.

315. नास्त्यलसस्य शास्त्राधिगमः ॥
A lazy man can never study the scriptures.

316. न स्त्रैणस्य स्वर्गाप्तिर्धर्मकृत्यं च ॥
An effeminate man can never complete any religious duty or go to heaven.

317. स्त्रियोऽपि स्त्रैणमवमन्यन्ते ॥
Even a woman abhors an effeminate man.

318. न पुष्पार्थी सिञ्चति शुष्कतरुम् ॥
A man who desires flowers would never irrigate a dry plant.

319. अद्रव्यप्रयत्नो वालिकाक्वाथनादनन्यः ॥
It is useless to perform a task without making any financial investment; it is similar to trying to extract oil from sand.

320. न महाजनहासः कर्तव्यः ॥
Wise people should never be ridiculed. They should always be treated with honour.

321. कार्यसम्पदं निमित्तानि सूचयन्ति ॥
The indications of doing a job provide the information about its eventual success or failure.

322. नक्षत्रादपि निमित्तानि विशेषयन्ति ॥
Stars can also predict the potential failure or success of the contemplated job.
323. न त्वरितस्य नक्षत्रपरीक्षा ॥
The person who is driven to succeed in their career disregards the stars' or planets' positions.
324. परिचये दोषा न छद्मन्ते ॥
Mere introduction can't reveal one's flaws.
325. स्वयमशुद्धः परानाशङ्कते ॥
He who is impure worries the most about others' impurity.
326. स्वभावो दुरतिक्रमः ॥
One's basic nature cannot be changed.
327. अपराधानुरूपो दण्डः ॥
The assigned punishment must be in tandem with the committed crime.
328. प्रश्नानुरूपं प्रतिवचनम् ॥
A response must conform to the foundational remark.
329. विभवानुरूपमाभरणम् ॥
One must carry ornaments which match the opulence level.
330. कुलानुरूपं वृतम् ॥
One's character must conform to the standard of the reputation of his clan.
331. कार्यानुरूपः प्रयत्नः ॥
Efforts must be measured according to the requirement of the job undertaken.
332. पात्रानुरूपं दानम् ॥
Charity must be made according to the needs of the receiver.
333. वयोऽनुरूपओ वेषः ॥
One's dress must be according to his age.

334. स्वाम्यनुकूलो भृत्यः ॥
A servant should always follow the orders of his master.

335. भतृवशवर्तिनी भार्या ॥
A wife must act according to her husband's desires.

336. गुरुवशानुवर्ती शिष्यः ॥
The disciple must always follow the mentor's commands.

337. पितृवशानुवर्ती पुत्रः ॥
A son should always be obedient to his father.

338. अत्युपचारः शङ्कितव्यः ॥
Behaving with excessive formalities raises suspicion about true intentions.

339. स्वामिनि कुपिते स्वामिनमेवानुवर्तेत ॥
A servant should follow the master's demands.

340. मातृताडितो वत्सो मातरमेवानुरोदिति ॥
A mother's punishment causes a youngster to sob solely in front of her. Since his mother's concern for his wellbeing is always evident, the youngster never criticizes her behaviour.

341. स्नेहवतः स्वल्पो हि रोषः ॥
Even the anger of well-wishers is regarded compassionate. They take firm action to get their child's poor behaviour properly corrected.

342. बालिशः आत्मछिद्रं न पश्यति अपि तु परच्छिद्रमेव पश्यति ॥
A fool always concentrates on finding faults in others and not in his own self.

343. सदोपचारः कितवः ॥
The scoundrels who are slaves always work with dishonest intentions.

344. काम्यैर्विशेषैरूपचारमुपचारः ॥
These scoundrels show their services by offering gifts the master specially likes.

345. चिरपरिचितानामत्युपचारः शङ्कितव्यः ॥

The display of extra honour by known people evokes a genuine suspicious.

346. श्वसहस्रादेकाकिनी गौः श्रेयसी ॥

A foul-tempered cow is still better than having a thousand dogs.

347. श्वो मयूरादद्य कपोतो वरः ॥

Today's pigeon is better than having a peacock of tomorrow.

348. अतिसङ्गो दोषमुत्पादयति ॥

Extra affection breeds weaknesses.

349. सर्वं जयत्यक्रोधः ॥

He who has the capacity to control his anger can totally win over everyone.

350. यद्यपकारिणी कोपः कर्तव्यः तर्हि स्वकोपे एवकोपः कर्तव्यः ॥

Showcase your anger only after the wrong doer expresses his anger at being exposed.

351. मतिमत्सु मूर्खमित्रगुरुवल्लभेषु विवादो न कर्तव्यः ॥

Never argue with the wise, the fools, the friends, the mentor and the master.

352. नास्त्यपिशाचमैश्वर्यम् ॥

Opulence is not devoid of evils.

353. नास्ति धनवतां सुकर्मसु श्रमः ॥

The wealthy never engage in selfless service. Because they constantly aim to make money from their actions.

354. नास्ति गतिश्रमो यानवताम् ॥

Those who are dependent upon vehicles never exert themselves by walking on foot.

355. यो यस्मिन् कर्मणि कुशलः स तस्मिन् योक्तव्यः ॥

He who excels in a specific field should be given a job within that field itself.

356. गुरूणां माता गरीयसी ॥

One's mother is the best teacher.

357. सर्वावस्थासु माता भर्तव्या ॥
Devotedly take care of your mother regardless of the conditions.

358. वैरूप्यमलङ्काकारेणाच्छाद्यते ॥
Outward decoration covers one's erudite knowledge.

359. विप्राणां भूषणं वेदः ॥
Knowledge of the Vedas act as a Brahman's jewel.

360. सर्वेषां भूषणं धर्मः ॥
Dharma is the original jewel for everyone.

361. अनुपद्रवं देशमावसेत् ॥
Always live in a country which is free from riots and any anarchy.

362. साधुजनबहुलो देशः आश्रयणीयः ॥
The country which can be dwelled in is that which has a majority of noble men.

363. राज्ञो भेतव्यं सार्वकालम् ॥
A king should always be feared.

364. न राज्ञः परं दैवतम् ॥
A king is the greatest diety.

365. सुदूरमपि दहति राजवह्निः ॥
The wrath of a king is a strong fire that burns the evil even in a far-off region.

366. रिक्तहस्तो न हाजानमभिगच्छेत् ॥
Never visit your king empty handed.

367. गुरुं दैवे च ॥
Never visit your Guru or temple with empty handed.

368. कुटिम्बिनो भेतव्यम् ॥
Never develop a grudge with the royal family.

369. गन्तव्यं च सदा राजकुलम् ॥
Visit the royal family frequently.

370. राजपुरुषैः सम्बन्धं कुर्यात् ॥
Maintain cordial relationship with the royal personages.

371. न चक्षुषाऽपि राजानं निरीक्षेत ॥
While standing before the king, never look in his eyes.

372. पुत्रे गुणवति कुटुम्बिनः स्वर्गः ॥
A virtuous son of a family makes all his family members happy.

373. पुत्रा विद्यानां पारं गमचितव्याः ॥
Hence, the son should be well-versed in a variety of fields and subjects.

374. जनपदार्थं ग्रामं त्यजेत् ॥
Sacrifice of a village can be practiced to ensure a region's or a country's welfare.

375. ग्रामार्थं कुटुम्बस्त्यजते ॥
Sacrifice of a family can be practiced to ensure a village's welfare.

376. अतिलाभः पुत्रलाभः ॥
Begetting a son brings blessings.

377. दुर्गतेरयः पितरौ रक्षति स पुत्रः ॥
A real son is one who protects his parents from all the troubles.

378. यः कुलं प्रख्यापयति स पुत्रः ॥
An able son brings glory and happiness to the entire family.

379. उपस्थितविनाशः पथ्यवाक्यं न शृणोति ॥
The onset of doom doesn't let the potential victim pay heed to any advice.

380. नास्ति देहिनां सुखदुःखाभावः ॥
Pain and pleasure go hand in hand in the life of the mortal beings.

381. मातरमिव वत्साः सुखदुःखानि कर्तारमेवानुगच्छन्ति ॥
Like children follow their mother, similarly, pain and pleasure follow mortal beings.

382. तिलमात्रमप्युपकारं शैलमात्रं मन्यते साधुः ॥

A gentleman always considers a mole-like obligation as big as a mountain.

383. उपकारोऽनार्थष्वकर्तव्यः ॥

Never oblige a mean person.

384. प्रत्युपकारभयादनार्यः शत्रुर्भवति ॥

A mean person will never acknowledge an obligation to be a favour.

385. स्वल्पोपकारकृतेऽपि प्रत्युपकारं कर्तुमार्यो जागर्ति ॥

A gentleman doesn't feel comfortable till he has repaid even the smallest of obligations.

386. न कदाऽपि देवता मन्तव्या ॥

Never insult the deities.

387. न चक्षुषः समं ज्योतिरस्ति ॥

There is no light better than the one which helps the eyes see things.

388. चक्षुर्हि शरीरिणां नेता ॥

Eyes are the controller of the body of mortal beings.

389. अपचक्षुषः किं शरीरेण ॥

A body is worthless without eyes.

390. नाप्सु मूत्रं कुर्यात् ॥

Never urinate while in water.

391. न नग्नो जलं प्रविशेत् ॥

Never enter the water naked.

392. यथा शरीरं तथा ज्ञानम् ॥

As is one's body, so is one's knowledge.

393. यथा बुद्धिस्तथा विभवः ॥

One's prosperity is directly proportional to one's wisdom.

394. अग्नावग्निं न निङ्पेत् ॥

Never fuel fire to the raging fire.

395. तपस्विनः पूजनीयाः ॥

Ascetics should always be venerated.

396. न वेदबाह्यो धर्मः ॥

Knowledge of dharma is a fundamental part of the Veda's teachings.

397. कथंचिदपि धर्मं निषेवेत ।।

One should act according to one's dharma.

398. स्वर्गं नयति सूनृतम् ।।

Honest conduct ensures one's place in heaven.

399. नास्ति सत्यात् परं तपः ।।

No penance is more merit bestowing than following truth.

400. सत्यं स्वर्गस्य साधनम् ।।

Following the path of truth is the means to gain heaven.

401. सत्येन धार्यते लोकः ।।

Truthfulness helps one survive in a society.

402. सत्याद्देवो वर्षति ।।

Truthfulness can make even the deities happy.

403. नानृतात् पातकं परम् ।।

No sin is deadlier than telling lies.

404. न मीमांस्या गुरवः ।।

Never criticize your guru.

405. खलत्वं नोपेयात् ।।

Never use evil tactics to accomplish your goal. In all circumstances, always choose the right course.

406. नास्ति खलस्य मित्रम् ।।

A wicked person has no friends.

407. लोकयात्रा दरिद्रं बाधते ।।

The poor don't benefit from living a material life in any way. For them, simply surviving each minute is a struggle.

408. अतिशूरो दानशूरः ।।

A charitable man is actually a brave man. Giving charity requires making certain sacrifices in order to fulfil the needs of others. Indeed, this was a supremely brave act.

409. गुरुदेवब्राह्मणेषु भक्तिर्भूषणम् ॥

Devotion towards Guru, Deity and Brahmans is the crown-jewel of all devotions.

410. सर्वस्य भूषणं विनयः ॥

Humility is the crowinging virtue.

411. अकुलीनोऽपि विनीतः कुलीनात्विशिष्टः ॥

Better than an unpleasant person from an aristocratic family is a courteous person of poor origin. Being born into a family is a gift from God, but in order to get respect in society after birth, one must learn to be humble.

412. आचारादायुर्वर्धते कीर्तिः श्रेयश्च ॥

Age and fame get enhanced by good conduct.

413. प्रियमप्यहितं न वक्तव्यम् ॥

The idea which is pleasant to listen but unfavourable in practice should not be uttered.

414. बहुजनविरुद्धमेकं नानुवर्तेत ॥

Don't follow one while having to desert many. Many can't collectively be wrong while one might be.

415. न दुर्जनेषु भाग्धेयः कर्तव्यः ॥

Do not enter into a partnership with dishonest people.

416. न कृतार्थस्य नीचेषु सम्बन्धः ॥

Don't keep a relationship with cunning people, even if it could be advantageous for you. Any affiliation will only damage one's reputation. So, despite the allure of potential riches in their affiliation, stay away from such company.

417. ऋणशत्रुव्याधयो निःशेषाः कर्तव्याः ॥

Try to eradicate debt, enemies and diseases from your life. Even if there is still evidence of them, it may become a serious problem.

418. भूत्यनुवर्तनं पुरुषस्य रसायनम् ॥

Affluence and wealth are the life's elixir for a man. Financial stability and physical comforts aid in maintaining good health.

419. नार्थिष्ववज्ञा नरकान्निवर्तनम् ॥

A beggar or someone begging for a favour should never be insulted or shown contempt to.

420. दुष्करं कर्म कारयित्वा कर्तारमवमन्यते नीचः ॥

A cruel person might make an expert suffer by assigning him a task that is extremely challenging. A nasty individual will continually try to cause difficulties and minimize others' accomplishments.

421. नाकृतज्ञस्य नरकान्निवर्तनम् ॥

There is no place except hell for an ungrateful person.

422. जिह्वायत्तौ वृद्धिविनाशौ ॥

One's development or destruction primarily depends upon one's speech.

423. विषयामृतयोराकरी जिह्वा ॥

The tongue can be used to deliver poison or nectar. If one is cautious in his speech, the listener will receive nectar; otherwise, poison.

424. प्रियवादिनो न शत्रुः ॥

A man with a sweet speech has no enemy.

425. स्तुता अपि देवतास्तुष्यन्ति ॥

Even the gods become ecstatic listening to their praise.

426. अनन्तमपि दुर्वचनं चिरं तिष्ठति ॥

Even the baseless remarks which are foul remain in one's memory.

427. राजद्विष्टं न वक्तव्यम् ॥

One should not make allegations against the king.

428. श्रुतिसुखात् कोकिलानापादपि तुष्यन्ति जनाः ॥

Those who enjoy listening to pleasant sweet notes will be pleased by the cuckoo's cooing.

429. स्वधर्महेतुः सत्पुरुषः ॥
Noble men's behaviour reveals the fundamental purpose of their religious faith.

430. नास्त्यर्थिनो गौरवम् ॥
An intense passion for money brings no honour. Misers who obsess over their money are often condemned by society.

431. स्त्रीणां भूषणं सौभाग्यम् ॥
Good fortune is the best jewel for women.

432. शत्रोरपि न पातनीय वृत्तिः ॥
Even the enemy's source of income for livelihood shouldn't be destructed.

433. अप्रयत्नोदकं क्षेत्रम् ॥
The location where a supply of water is easily accessible should be one's permanent residence. Water is necessary for existence in a tropical nation like India. If one needs to go through tremendous hardships to obtain it, the pleasant stay and prosperity will suffer.

434. एरण्डमवलम्ब्य कुञ्जरं न कोपयेत् ॥
Never invite the wrath of the powerful on getting the support of a weakling.

435. अतिप्रवृद्धापि शाल्मली वारणस्तम्भो न भवति ॥
An elephant cannot be tied to an old Saal tree. A Saal tree is normally fairly solid and powerful, but it cannot be used to tie an elephant to it when it has withered with age.

436. अतिदीर्घोऽपि कर्णिकारो न मुसली भवति ॥
The wood of an Okander tree, no matter how large, cannot be utilized to manufacture a hammer. The size alone cannot guarantee the quality of the contents.

437. अतिदीप्तोऽपि खद्योतो न पावकः ॥
Even the intense glow can't turn a glow-worm into a

fire-fling.

438. न प्रवृद्धत्वं गुणहेतुः ॥

Excellence doesn't necessarily give rise to good qualities.

439. सुजीर्णोऽपि पुचुमल्दो न शङ्कुलायते ॥

A nut-cutter cannot be made from a neem tree, no matter how old it is. Although the wood of the neem tree is exceedingly tough and grows stronger with age, it cannot replace the iron necessary to build a nut-cutter.

440. यथा बीजं तथा निष्पत्तिः ॥

One reaps as one sows.

441. यथा श्रुतं तथा बुद्धिः ॥

One's intelligence is conditioned by what one listens to.

442. यथा कुलं तथाऽऽचारम् ॥

One gets his foundational characteristics in accordance with the family pedigree.

443. संस्कृतः पिचुमन्दो न सहकारो भवति ॥

Regardless of how much a neem-tree ripens, it can never transform into a mango tree.

444. न चागतं सुखं त्यजेत् ॥

One shouldn't let go of the available pleasure in hope of enjoying a bigger one in future.

445. स्वयमेव दुःखमधिगच्छति ॥

A man invites his miseries himself.

446. रात्रिचारणं न कुर्यात् ॥

Never wander aimlessly at night.

447. न चार्धरात्रं स्वपेत् ॥

Sleeping at the odd hour of mid-night is not advisable.

448. तद्विद्विद्भिः परीक्षेत ॥

Talk to scholars to know more about God.

449. परगृहमकारणतो न प्रविशेत् ॥

Don't enter someone else's house without any sincere reason.

450. ज्ञात्वाऽपि दोषमेव करोति लोकः ॥

People commit crimes knowingly.

451. शास्त्रप्रधाना लोकवृत्तिः ॥

Social conduct is regulated by divine knowledge.

452. शास्त्राभावे शिष्टाचारमनुगच्छेत् ॥

Where scriptural dictates are not present, follow social customs.

453. नाचरिताच्छस्त्रं गरीयः ॥

Scriptures don't get precedence over social customs.

454. दूरस्थमपि चाचक्षुः पश्यति राजा ॥

A king's intelligence network allows him to predict or investigate a distant scenario.

455. गतानुगतिको लोकः ॥

After seeing others' behaviour, one adopts their behaviour. People typically follow mindlessly rather than carefully consider their options; they have a repeatative attitude. But those who utilize their brains while also paying attention to other people's behaviour typically succeed more often in their endeavours.

456. यमनुजीवेत् तं नापवदेत् ॥

Never criticize the one on whose favour your survival depends.

457. तपस्सार इन्द्रियनिग्रहः ॥

The essence of all penances is practticing control over your senses.

458. यज्ञफलज्ञास्त्रिवेदविदः ॥

The consequences of sacrifice are known to those who are knowledgeable about the Vedic literature.

459. स्वर्गस्थानं न शाश्वतं अपि तु यानत्पुण्यफलम् ॥

One's position in heaven is not eternal.

460. न च स्वर्गपतनात् परं दुःखम् ॥
Fall from heaven gives one extreme sorrow.

461. देही देहं त्यक्त्वा ऐन्द्रपदं न वाञ्छति ॥
A living being wouldn't want to quit his body even if he is offered Indra's position in heaven.

462. दुःखानामौषधं निर्वाणम् ॥
Absolute emancipation (Nirvana) is the solution of all worldly miseries.

463. अनार्यसम्बन्धाद्वरमार्यशत्रुता ॥
A wise enemy is better than a foolish friend.

464. निहन्ति दुर्वचनं कुलम् ॥
Harsh words can even destroy a family.

465. विवादे धर्ममनुस्मरेत् ॥
In no discussion should one forget one's noble dictates.

466. निशान्ते कार्यं चिन्तयेत् ॥
Plan the course of action at dawn.

467. उपस्थितविनाशः दुर्नयं शुभं मन्यते ॥
One resorts to unjust measures when faced with doom.

468. न दानसमं वश्यम् ॥
There is no favour higher than indulging in charity.

469. परायत्तेषूत्कण्ठां न कुर्यात् ॥
Never desire for something which belongs to another.

470. अत्समृद्धिरसद्भिरेव भुज्यते ॥
Ill-earned money always gets consumed in ill-company.

471. निम्बफलं काकैर्हि भुज्यते ॥
The (bitter) neem-fruit is only consumed by crows (bad people).

472. नाम्भोधिस्तृष्णामपोहति ॥
Sea-water cannot quench someone's thirst.

473. वालिका अपि स्वगुणमाश्रयन्ते ॥
Sand also follows a defined conduct.

474. सन्तोऽसत्सु न रमन्ते ॥

Saintly people never enjoy the company of rogues.

475. हंसः प्रतवने न रमते ॥

(In continuation to the last shloka) A swan can't enjoy in a cremation ground.

476. अर्थार्थं प्रवर्तते लोकः ॥

The world works for accumulating financial gains.

477. आशया बध्यते लोकः ॥

Hope has the power to hold the world together.

478. न च आशापरैः श्री सह तिष्ठति ॥

Wealth does not stay with someone who only hopes but doesn't make any effort to acquire it.

479. आशापरे न धैर्यम् ॥

One can't develop patience if he hopes all the time.

480. दैन्यान्मरणमुत्तमम् ॥

Death is better than suffering in poverty.

481. आशालज्जां व्यपोहति ॥

Those who keep on only hoping and refuse to act are devoid of shame.

482. आत्मा न स्तोतव्यः ॥

One should not praise oneself.

483. न दिवा स्वप्नं कुर्यात् ॥

One should avoid sleeping during the day time.

484. न चासन्नपि पश्यत्यैश्वर्यान्धः नापि श्रृणोतीष्टं वाक्यम् ॥

A man blinded by the lust for money doesn't listen to sane advice.

485. अतिथिअभ्यागतं च पूजयेद्यथाविधि ॥

Give as much respect to a guest in your home as possible.

486. नास्ति हव्यस्य व्याघातः ॥

No noble act goes to waste or unrewarded.

487. शत्रुर्मित्रवत् प्रतिभाति ॥

An enemy appears as a friend when one's wisdom is clouded.

488. मृगतृष्णा जलवद्भाति हि ॥
The sand of a desert appears like the waving water (when the vision is clouded).
489. धुरमेधसोऽसच्छास्त्रं मोहयति ॥
Fools love the books which provide incorrect advice.
490. सत्सङ्गः स्वर्गवासः ॥
The company of the noble men makes one feel like he is dwelled in heaven.
491. आर्याः स्वमिव परं मन्वते ॥
The noblemen consider others equal to themselves.
492. रूपानुवर्ती गुणः ॥
Good qualities reflect on one's physical appearance.
493. यत्र सुखेन वर्तते तदेव स्थानम् ॥
The place where one gets happiness is a good place.
494. विश्वासघातिनो न निष्कृतिः ॥
A treacherous person never gets freedom (from guilty conscience).
495. दैवायत्तं न शोचेत् ॥
One shouldn't grieve about his misfortune.
496. आश्रितदुःखमात्मन इव मन्यते साधुः ॥
The noble men acknowledge their dependent's problems as their very own.
497. हृद्गतमाच्छाद्यान्यद्वदत्यनार्यः ॥
A cruel person will never express genuine sentiments in front of others and will constantly conceal their actual emotions.
498. बुद्धिहीनः पिशाचतुल्यः ॥
A man sans intelligence is a wretch.
499. सहायः पथि न गच्छेत् ॥
Don't follow a path where you get no support.
500. पुत्रो न स्तोतव्यः ॥
A son should never be praised on face.

501. स्वामी स्तोतव्योऽनुजीविभिः ॥
The servants should always praise their master.

502. धर्मकृत्यानि सर्वाणि स्वामिन इत्येव घोषयेत् ॥
The master, on whose orders the servants carry out the sacred rites, should receive the primary praise from them.

503. राजाज्ञां नातिलङ्घयेत् ॥
The royal order should never be violated.

504. यथाऽऽज्ञप्तं तथा कुर्यात् ॥
The royal order should be obeyed diligently.

505. नास्ति बुद्धिमतां शत्रुः ॥
The wise have no enemies.

506. आत्मछिद्रं न प्रकाशयेत् ॥
Never let anyone get to know your weakness.

507. क्षमावानेव सर्वं साधयति ॥
A forgiving person gets praise from everyone.

508. आपदर्थं धनं रक्षेत् ॥
Save money to protect yourself from distress.

509. साहसवतां प्रायं कर्तव्यम् ॥
Work is worship for a daring person.

510. श्वः कार्यमद्य कुर्वीत ॥
Do today's work today only. Work should not be postponed.

511. आपराह्णिकं पूर्वाह्ण एव कर्तव्यम् ॥
Complete the work meant for the morning in the morning itself.

512. व्यवहारानुलोमो धर्मः ॥
Acting in tandem with one's social norms corroborates adhering to one's religious faith.

513. सर्वज्ञता लोकज्ञता ॥
One who knows the world knows all.

514. शास्त्रज्ञोऽप्यलोकज्ञो मूर्खतुल्यः ॥

One who has the scriptural knowledge but no worldly knowledge is akin to a fool.

515. शात्रप्रयोजनं तत्त्वदर्शनम् ।।

The main purpose of scriptural knowledge is to find actual knowledge about all things.

516. तत्त्वज्ञानं कार्यमेव प्रकाशयति ।।

Work enlightens one about the real world knowledge.

517. व्यवहारे पक्षपातो न कर्तव्यः ।।

One should never have a discriminatory attitude towards anyone.

518. धर्मादपि व्यवहारो गरीयान् ।।

Social conduct is far more important than religious faith.

519. आत्मा हि व्यवहारस्य साक्षी ।।

One's soul is the sole witness of one's conduct.

520. सर्वसाक्षी ह्यात्मा ।।

One's soul is the universal witness.

521. न स्यात् कूटसाक्षी ।।

One should never be a false witness.

522. कूटसाक्षिणो नरके पतन्ति ।।

Every false witness goes to hell.

523. प्रच्छन्नपापानां साक्षिणो महाभूतानि ।।

The five elements: earth, air, water, fire, and ether, also witness the hidden acts of sin.

524. आत्मनः पापमात्मैव प्रकाशयति ।।

One's soul always gives away to one's own acts of sin.

525. व्यवहारोऽन्तर्गतमाकारः सूचयति ।।

One's character is identified by behaviour.

526. आकारसंवरणं देवानामप्यशक्यम् ।।

Human behaviour is reflected through face. Even the deities can't hide it.

527. चोरराजपुरुषेभ्यो वित्तं रक्षेत् ।।

Wealth should be saved from the royal men and thieves.

528. दुर्दर्शना हि राजानः प्रजा रक्षन्ति ॥

The king who is rarely to be seen often destroys the prosperity of his subjects.

529. सुदर्शना राजानः प्रजा रक्षन्ति ॥

The king who is easily accessible to his subjects keeps them happy.

530. न्याययुक्तं राजानं मातरं मन्यन्ते प्रजाः ॥

A just king is akin to a mother for the subjects.

531. तादृशः स राजा इह सुखं ततः स्वर्गण् चाप्नोति ॥

Such a king, as was said in the preceding sutra, gets paradise after death in addition to all the delights of this life.

532. अहिंसालक्षणो धर्मः ॥

Non-violence is the basic tenet of every religious faith.

533. स्वशरीरमपि परशरीरं मन्यते साधुः ॥

Holy men utilize their body for other's welfare as though the body is not their own.

534. मांसभक्षणमप्युक्तं सर्वेषाम् ॥

Eating flesh is bad for all.

535. न संसारभयं ज्ञानवताम् ॥

Wise people are not afraid of the world.

536. विज्ञानदीपेन संसारभयं निवर्तयति ॥

The lamp of scientific knowledge removes the fear of the world.

537. सर्वमवित्यं भवति ॥

Everything in this world is mortal.

538. कृमिशन्कृन्मूत्रभाचनं शरीरं पुण्यतयपापजन्महेतुः ॥

Why then must one have excessive affection for this body, which is ultimately simply a storehouse of urine and faeces and is responsible for all crimes and merits?

539. जन्ममरणादिषु तु दुःखमेव ॥

Sorrow is the end result of every birth and death.

540. तपसा स्वर्गमाप्नोति ॥

Only holy deeds can help one attain heaven.

541. क्षमायुक्तस्य तपो विवर्धते ॥

He who is forgiving by nature enhances religious austerity.

542. तस्मात् सर्वेषां सर्वकार्यसिद्धिर्भवति ॥

Being naturally forgiving, firm in faith, and committed to penance will ultimately lead to success in every endeavour.

◆